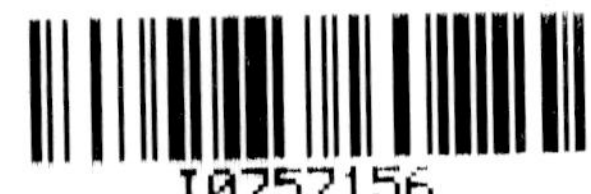

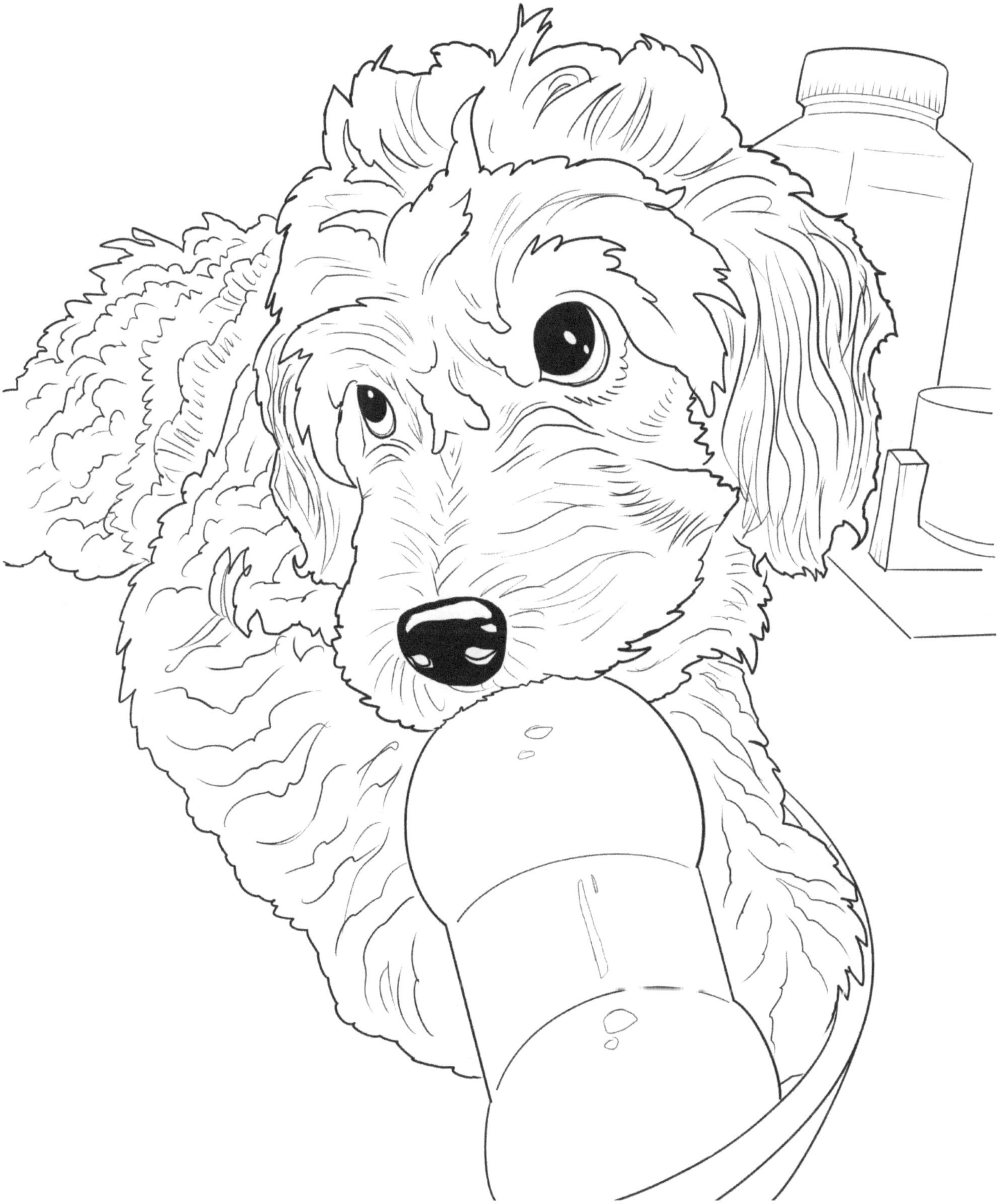

I0757156

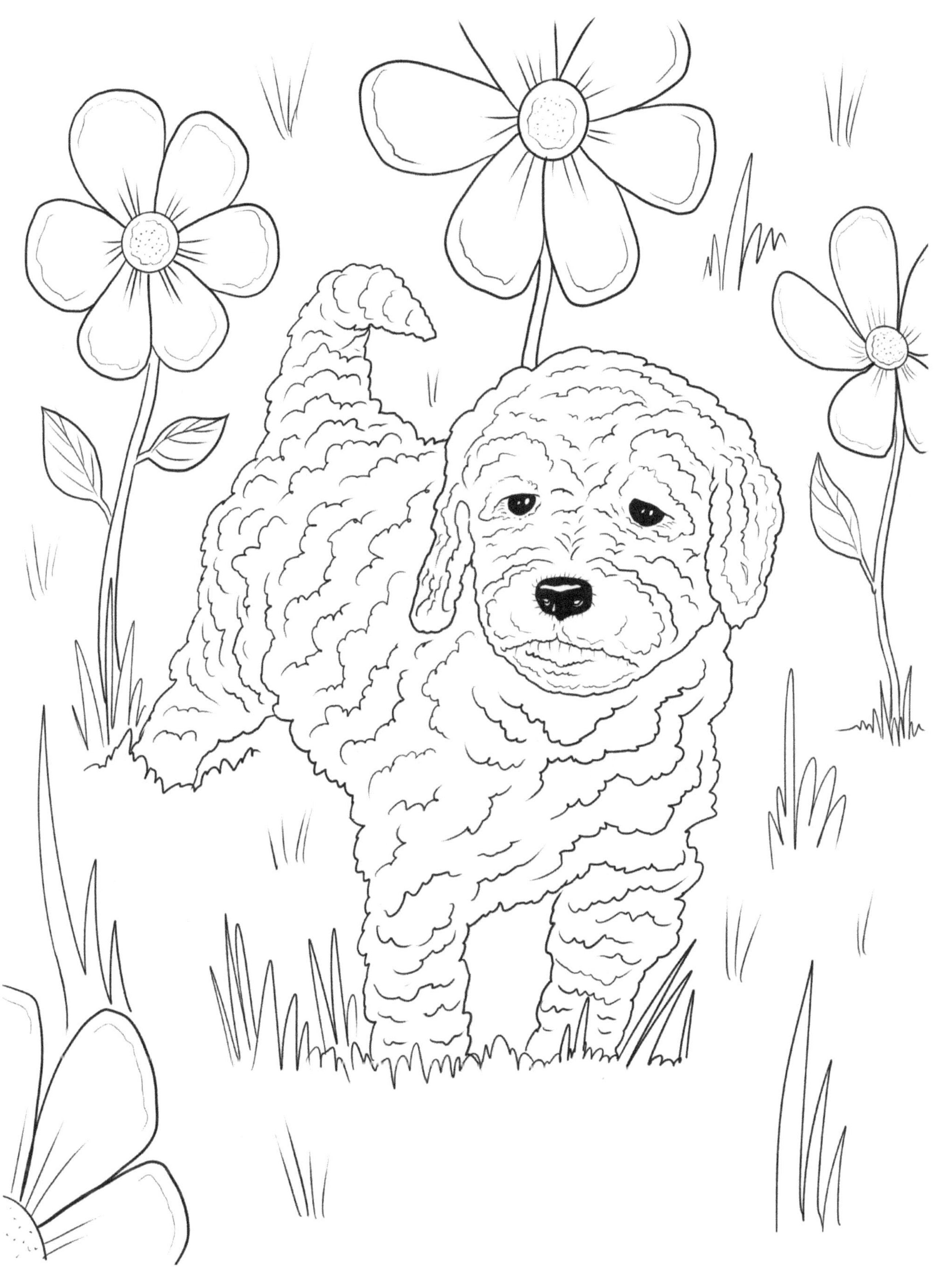

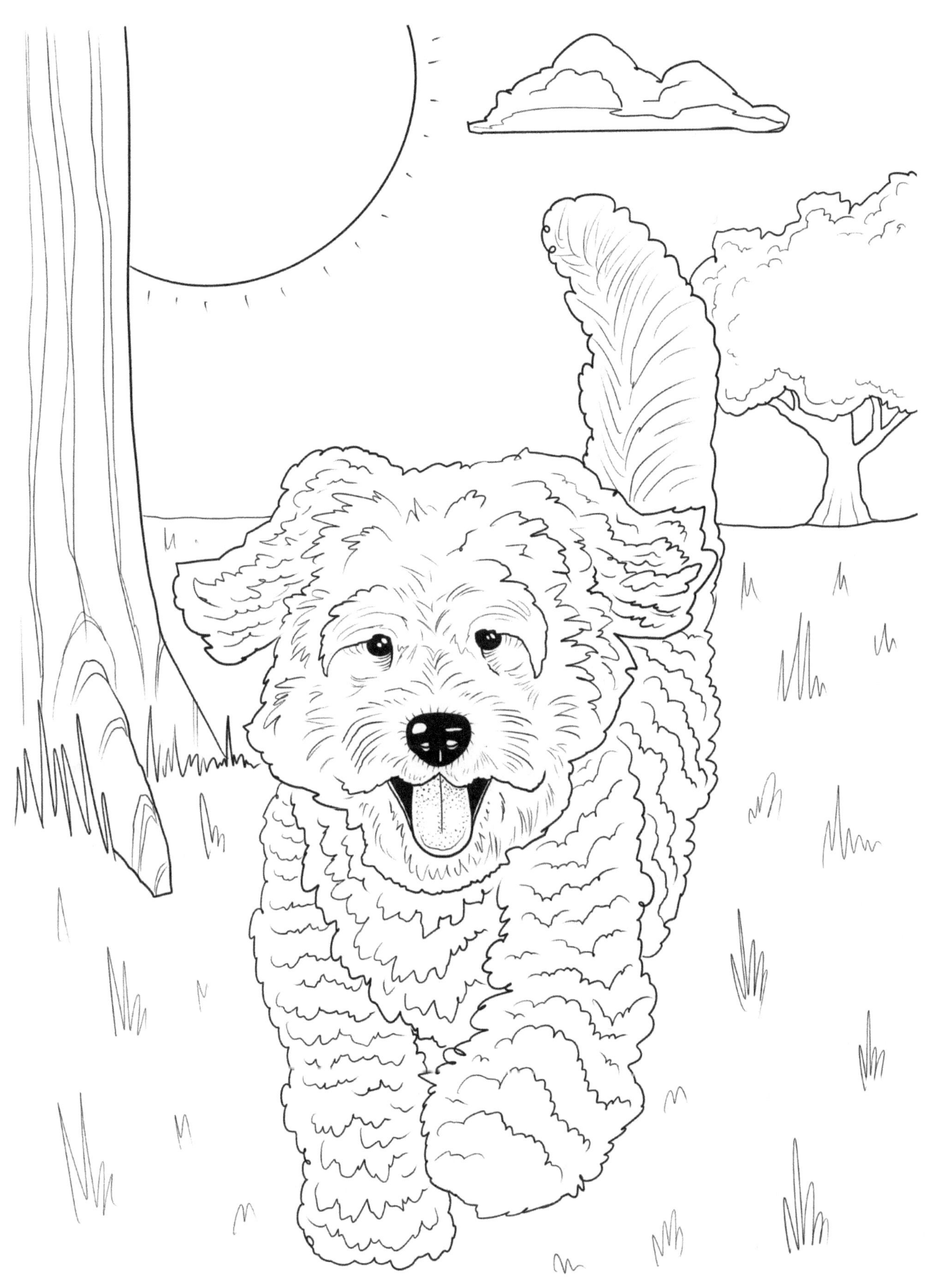

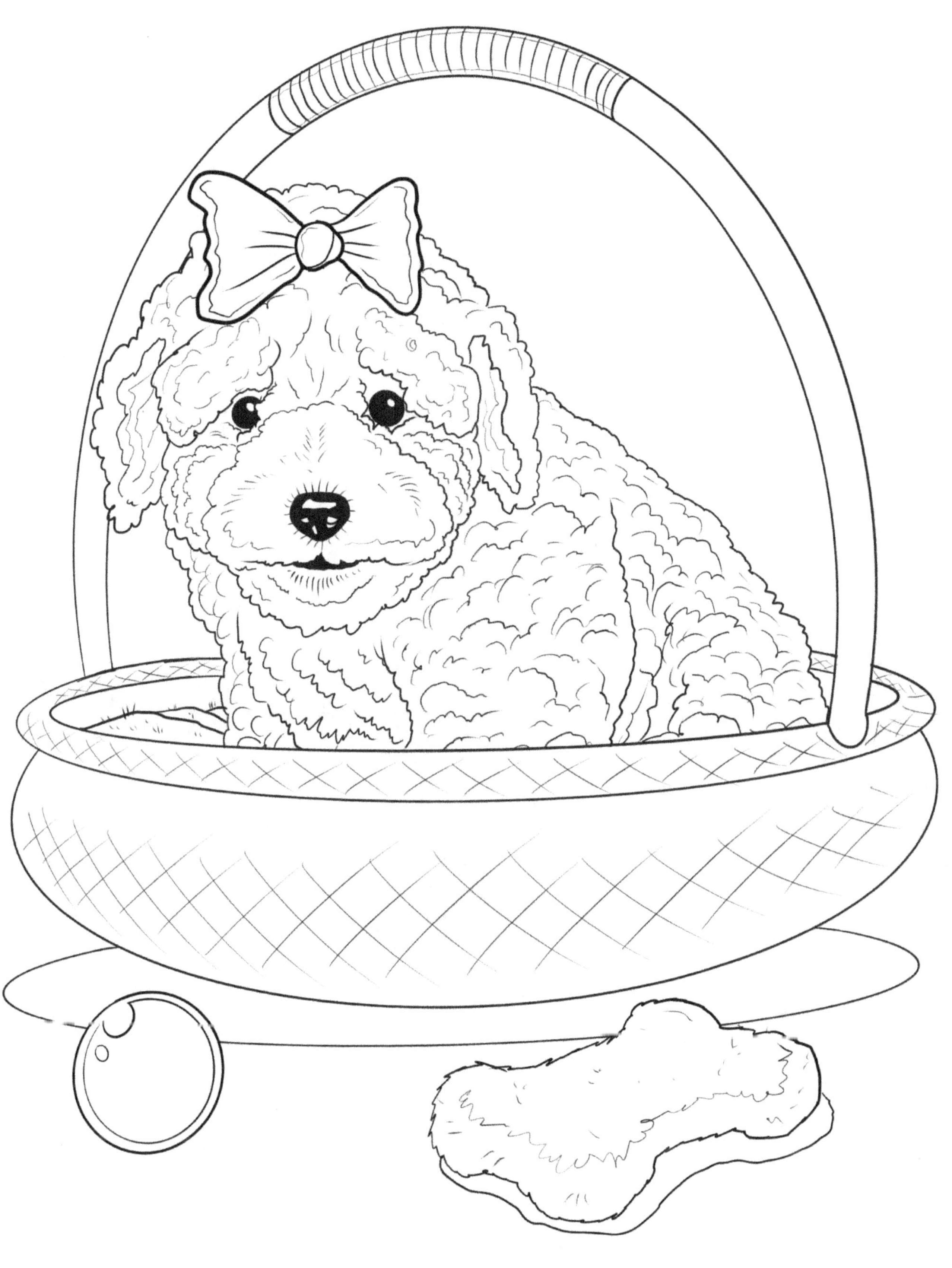

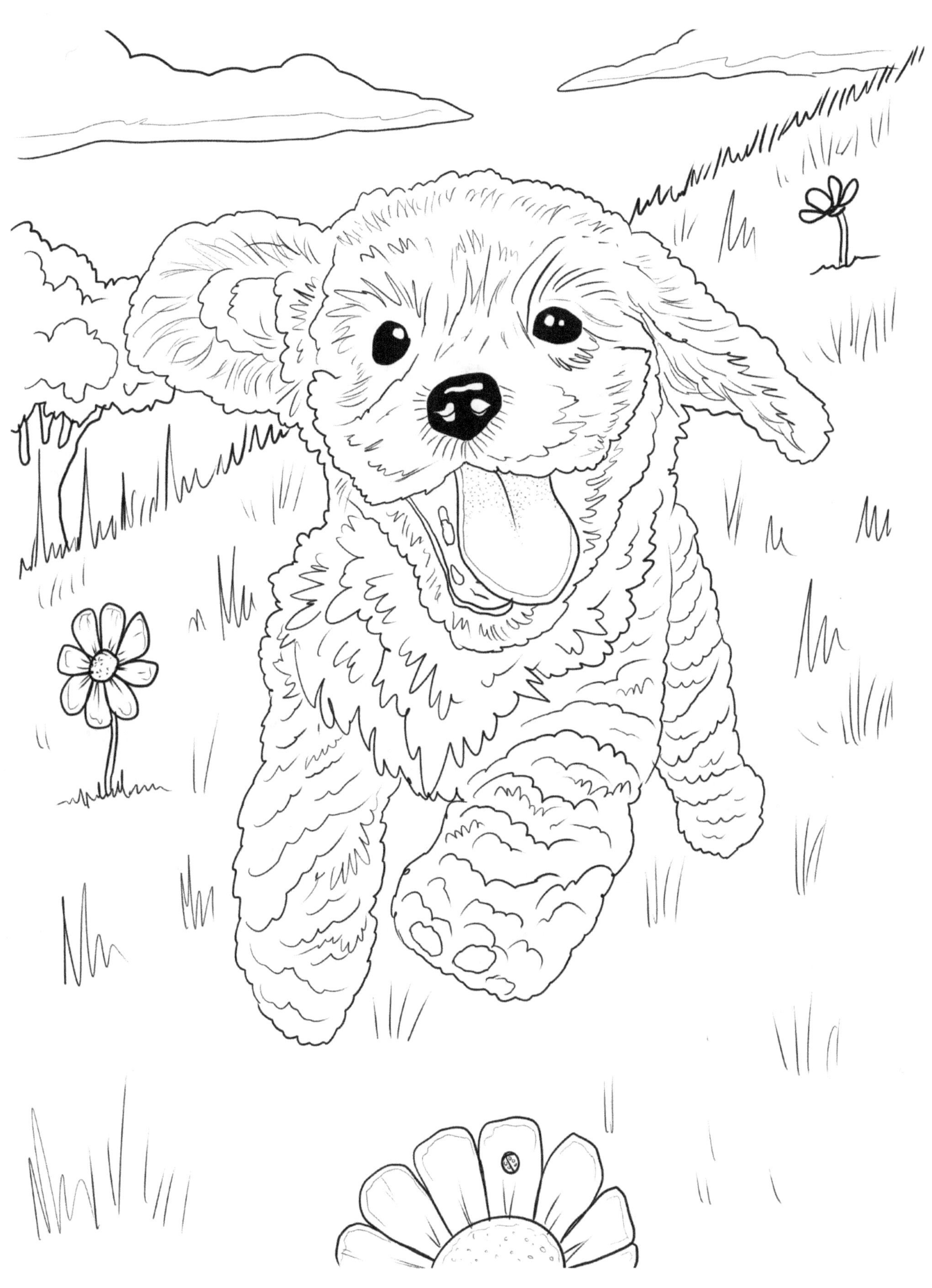

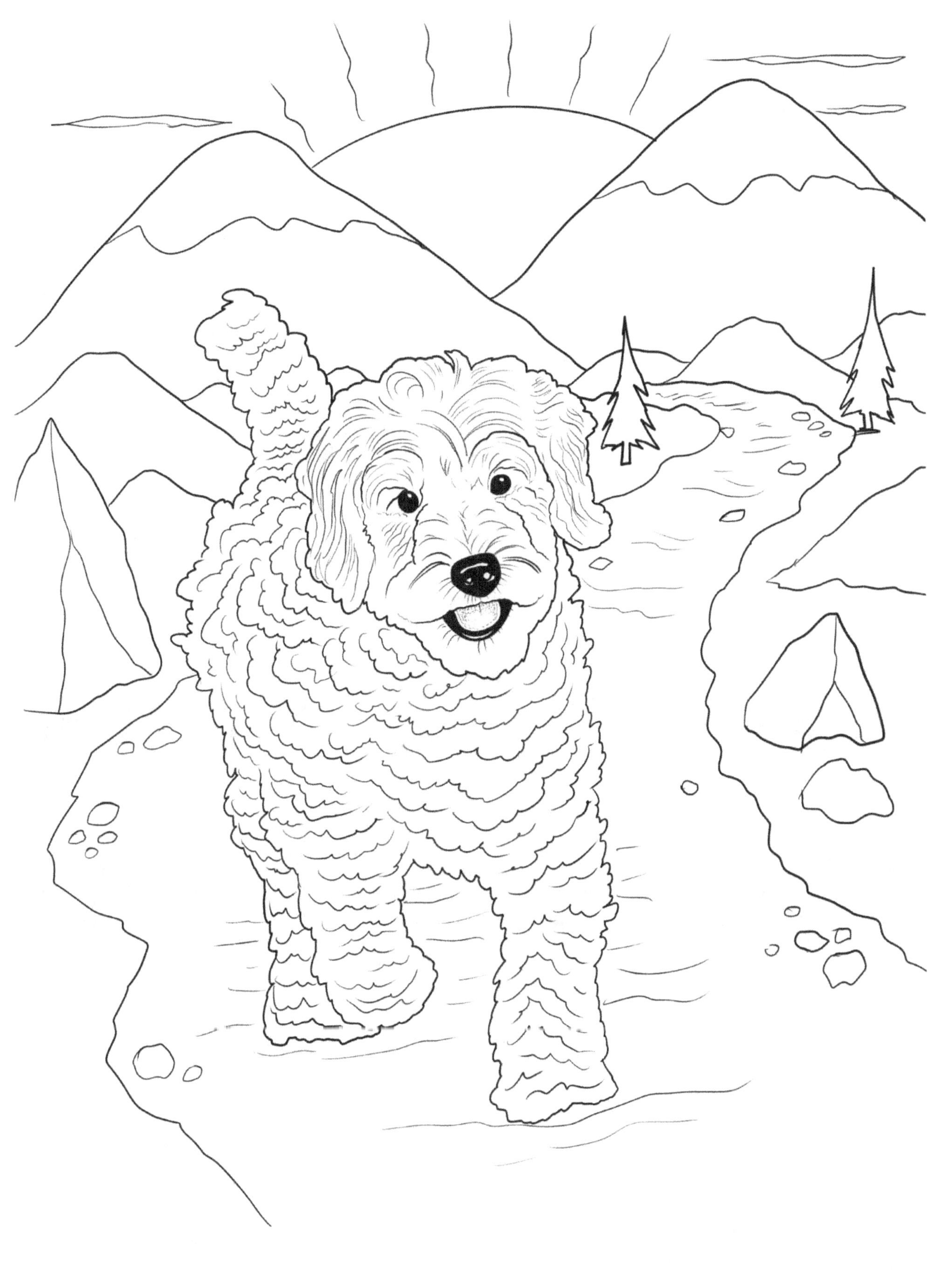

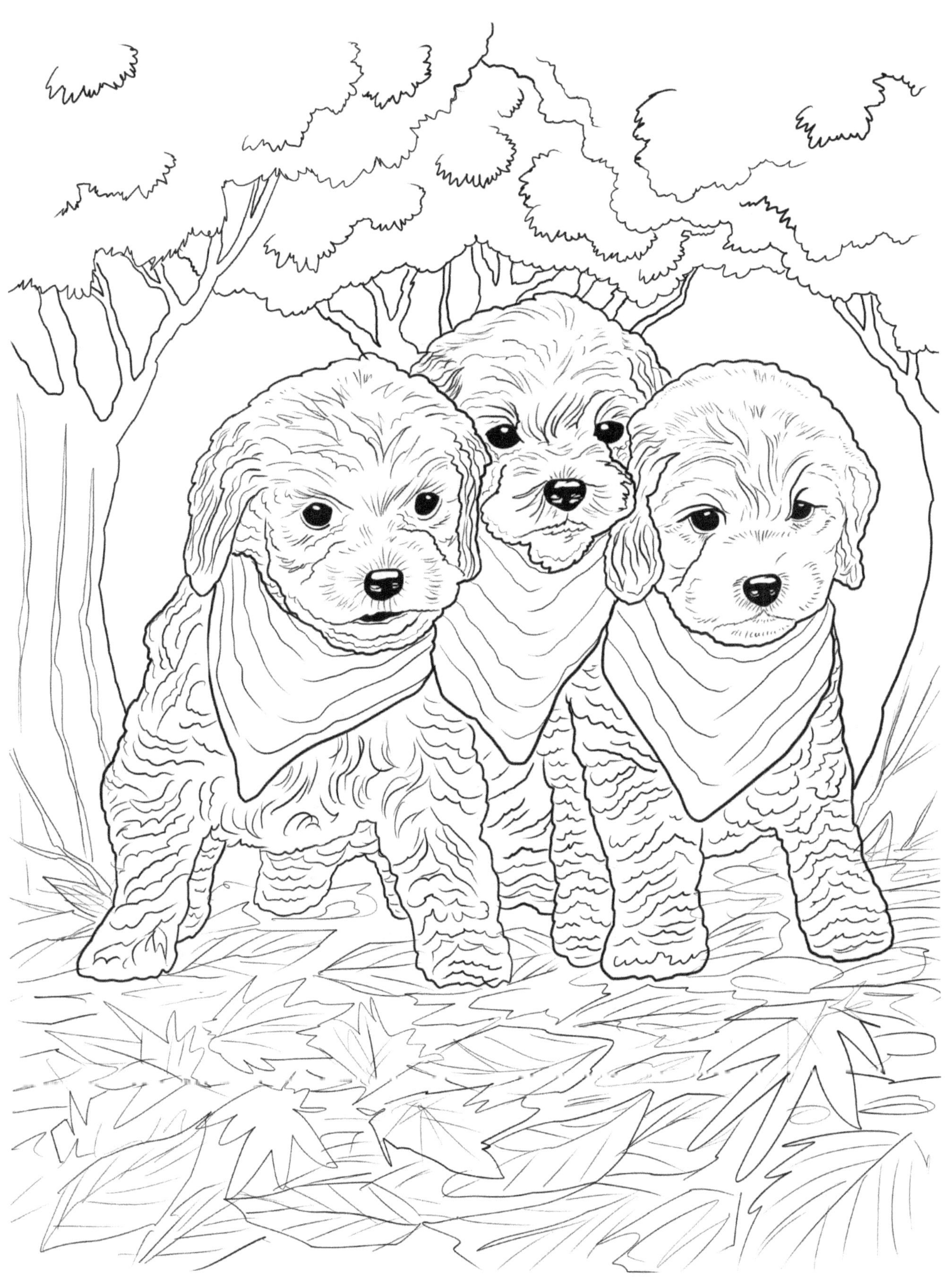

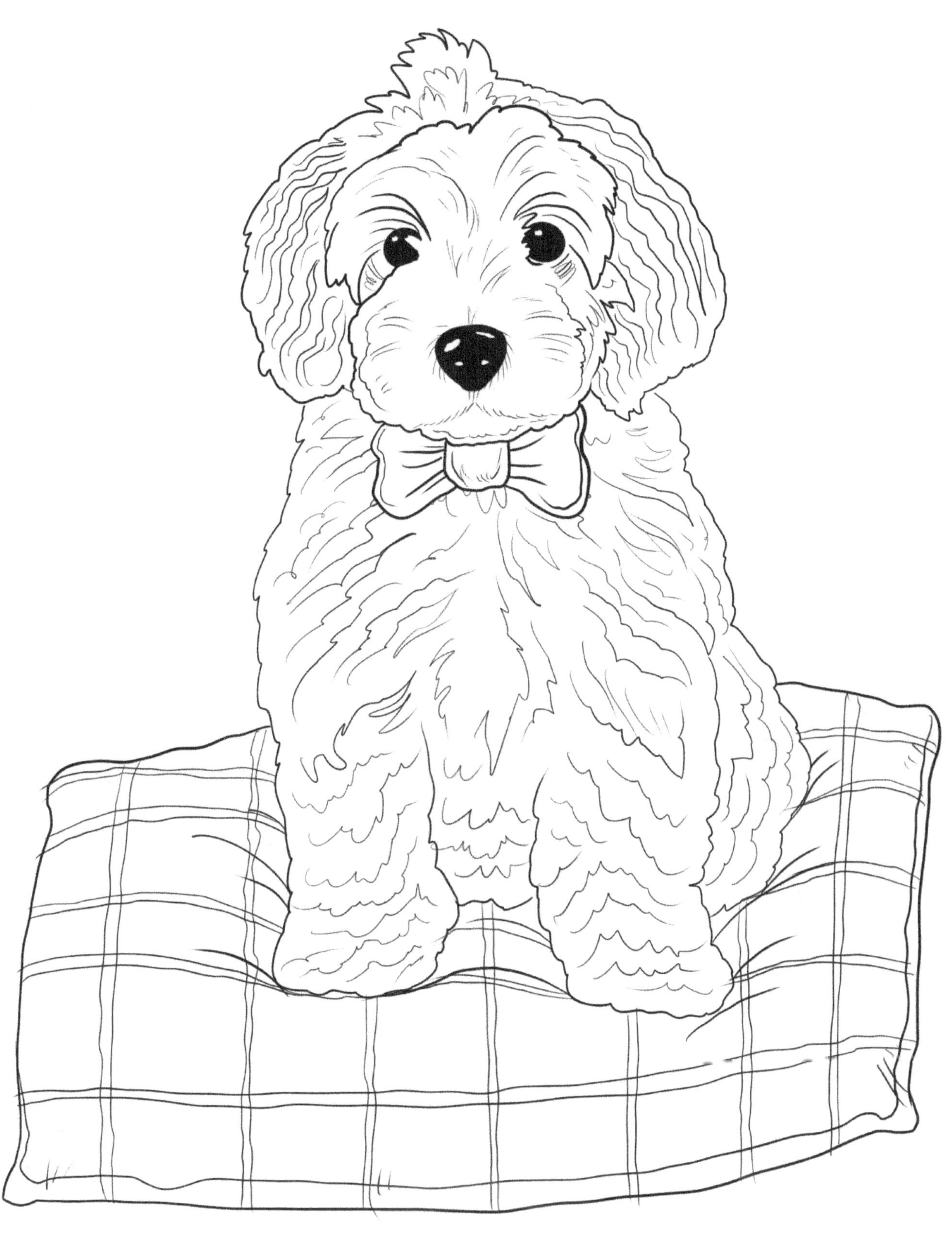

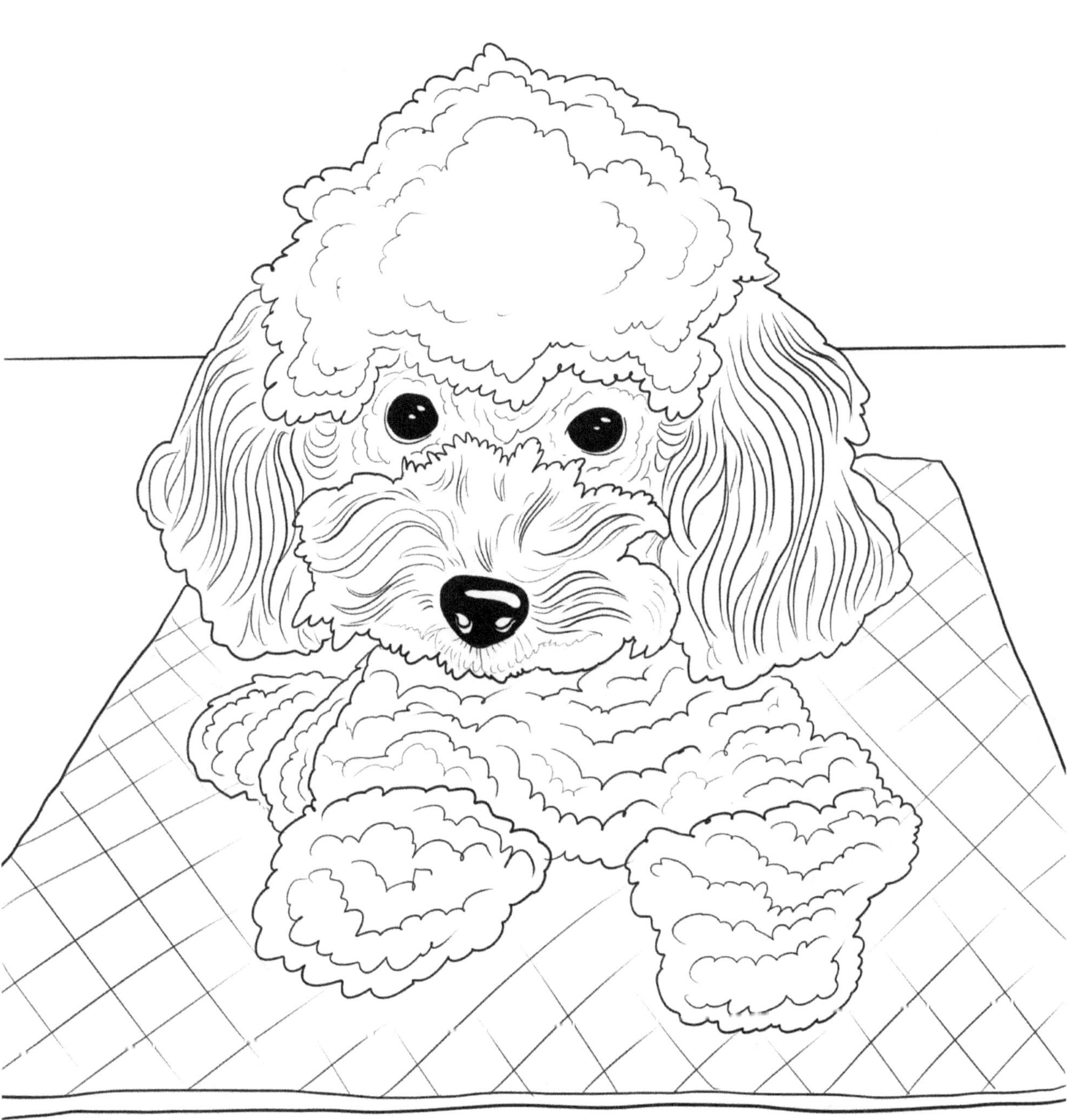

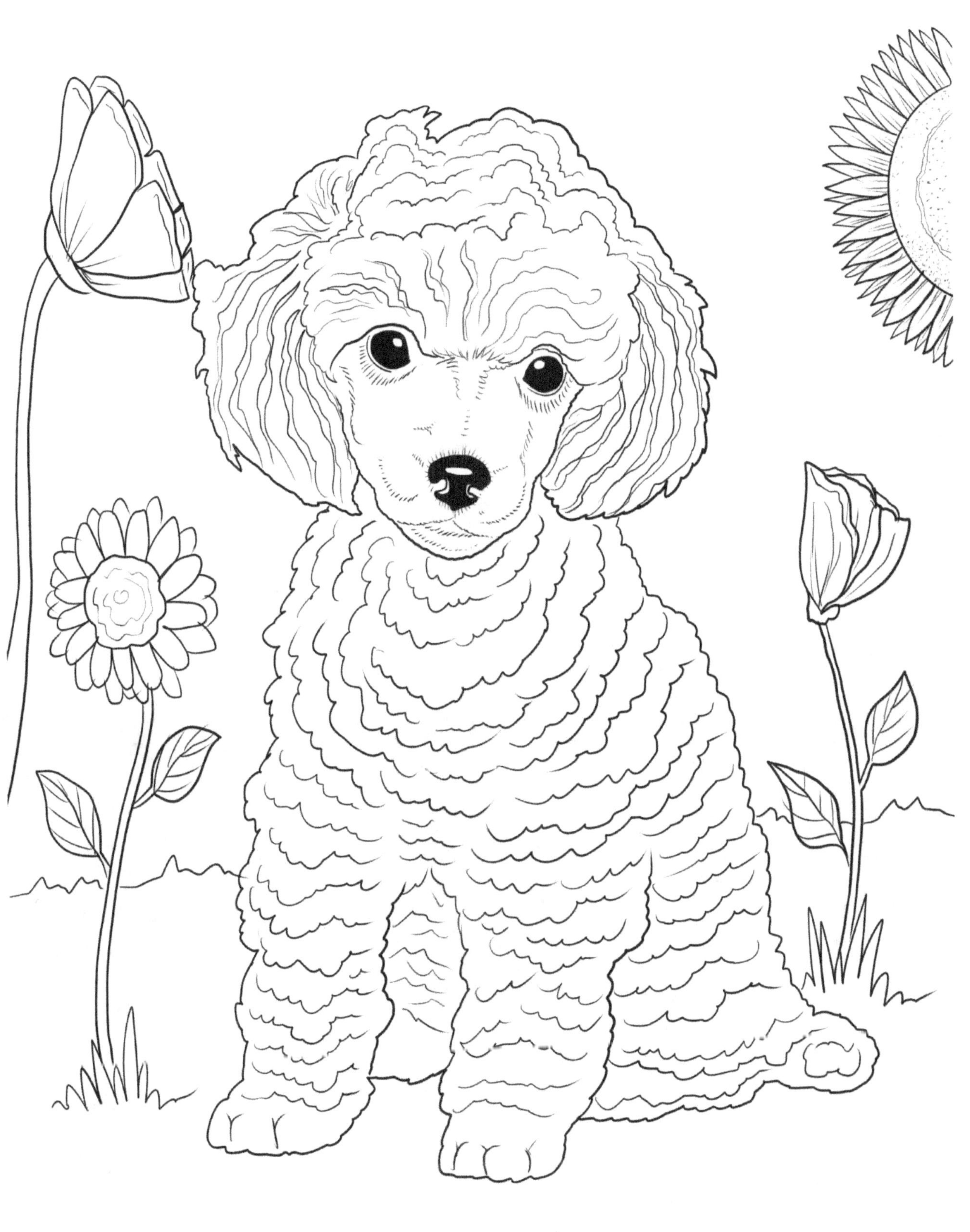

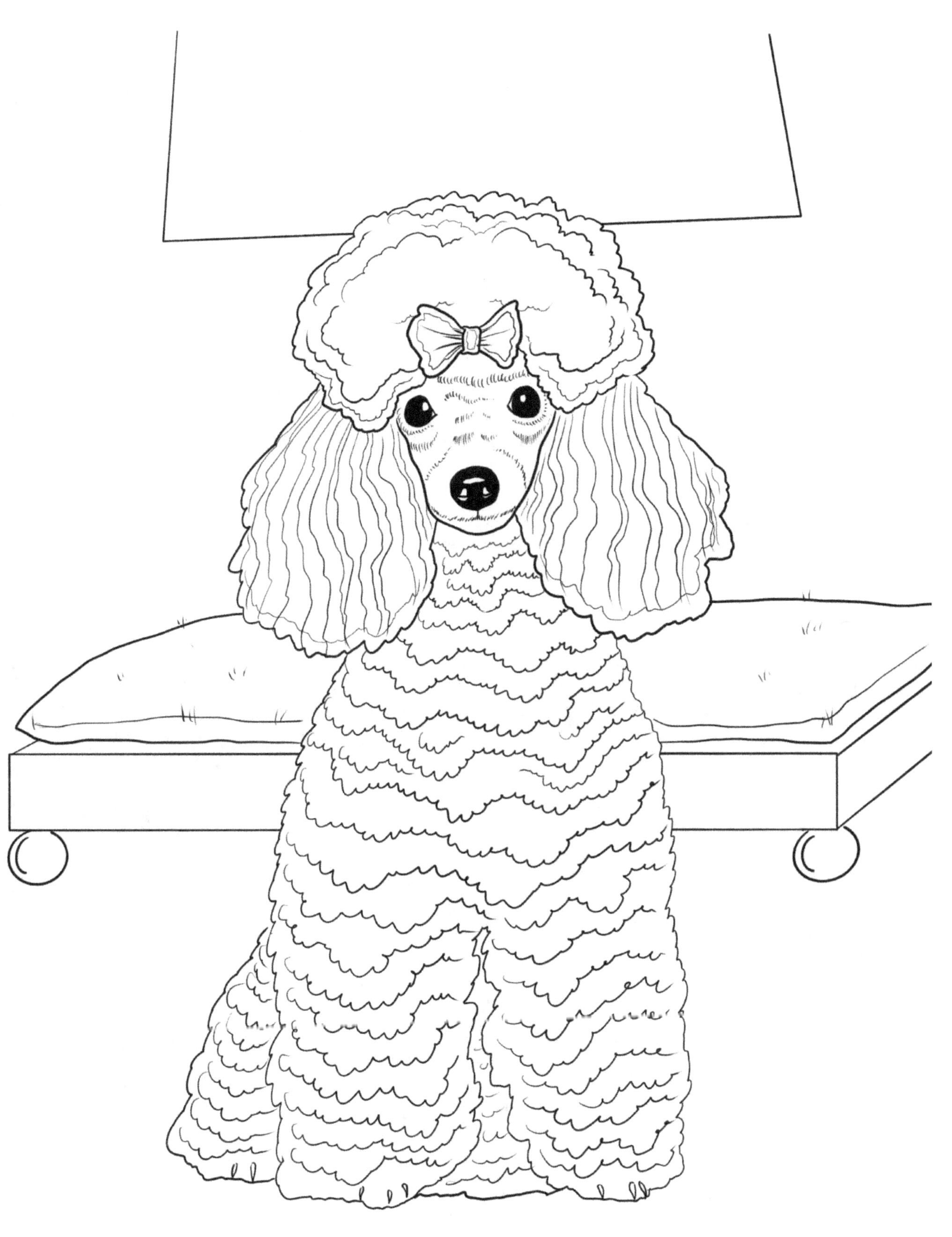

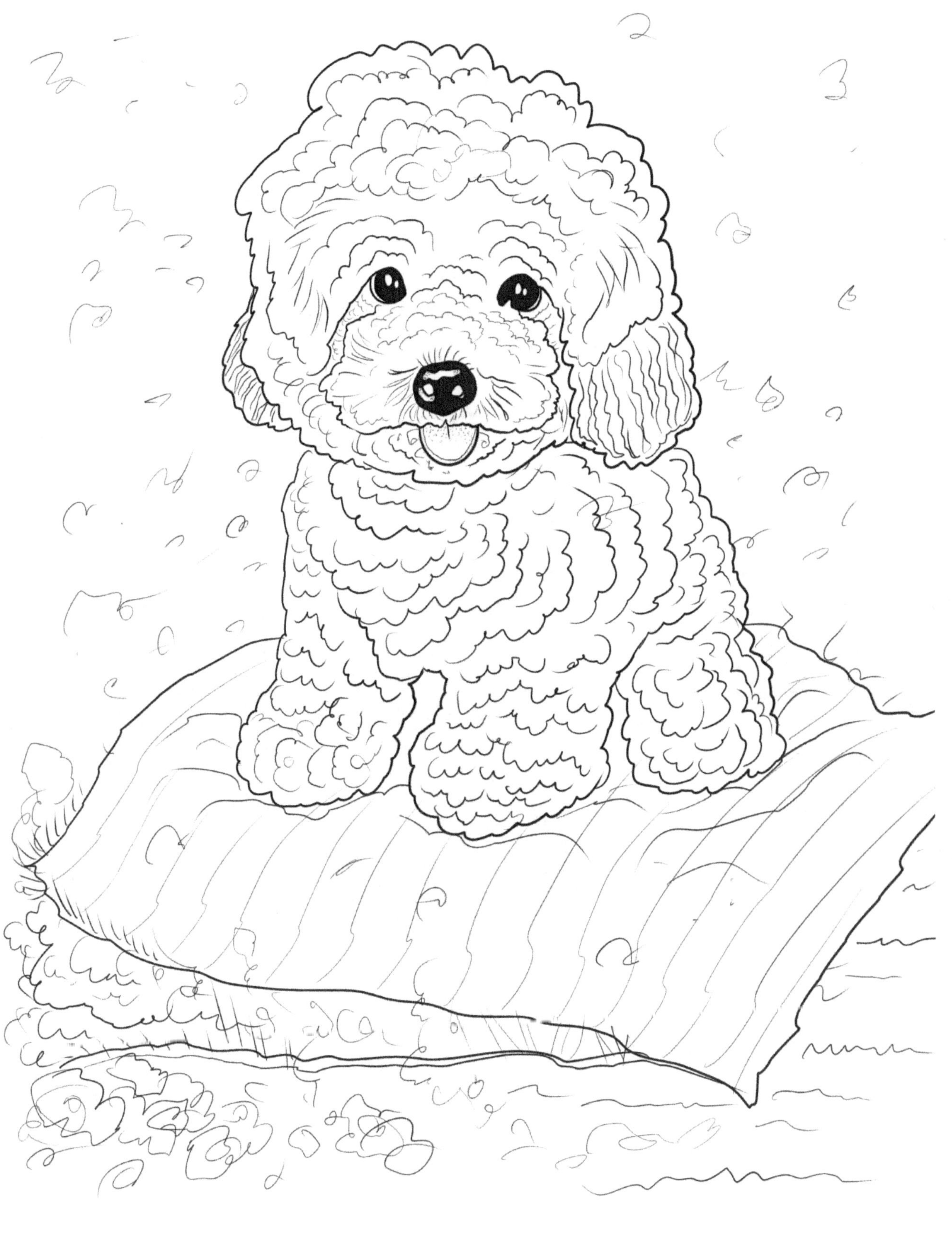

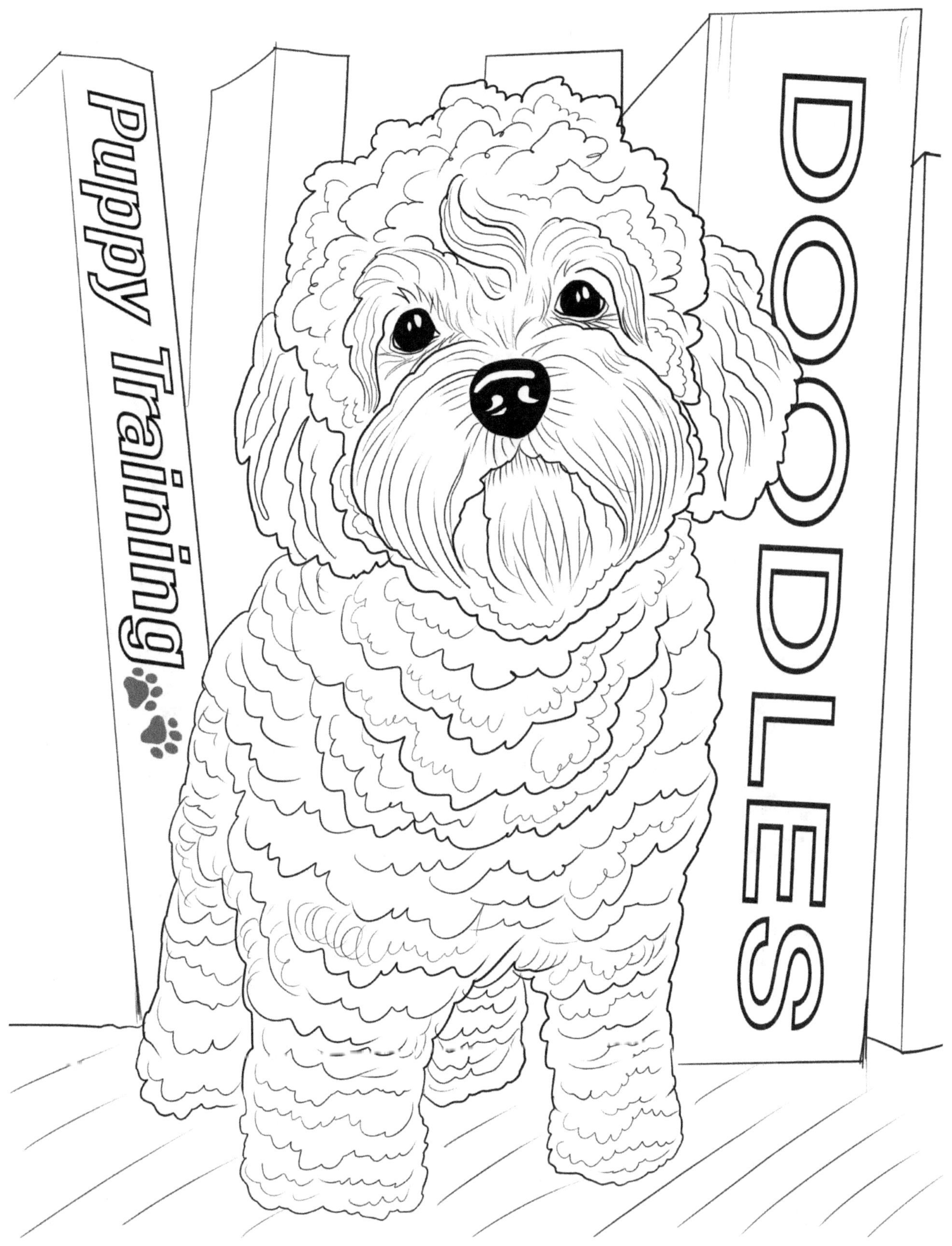

Puppy Training
DOODLES

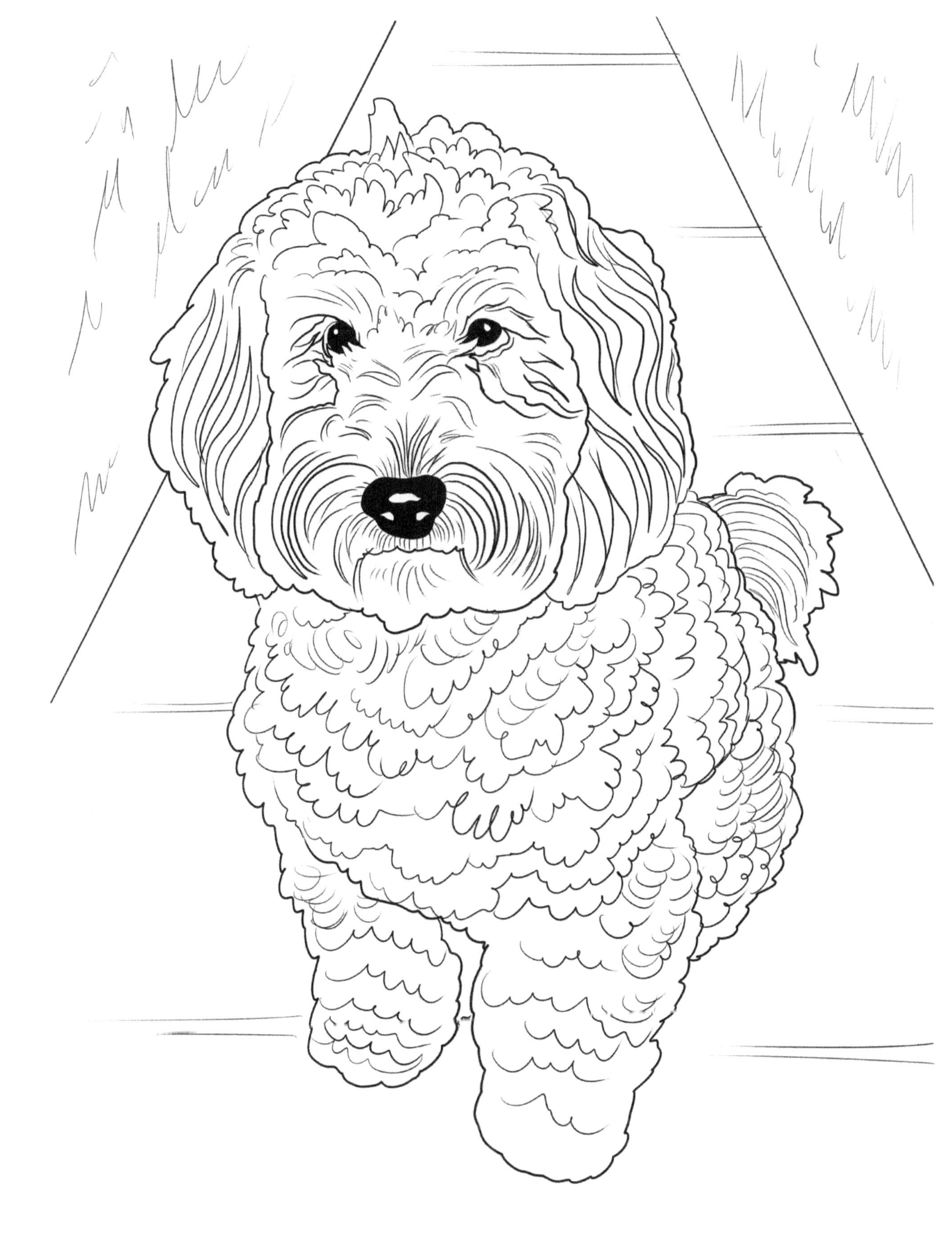

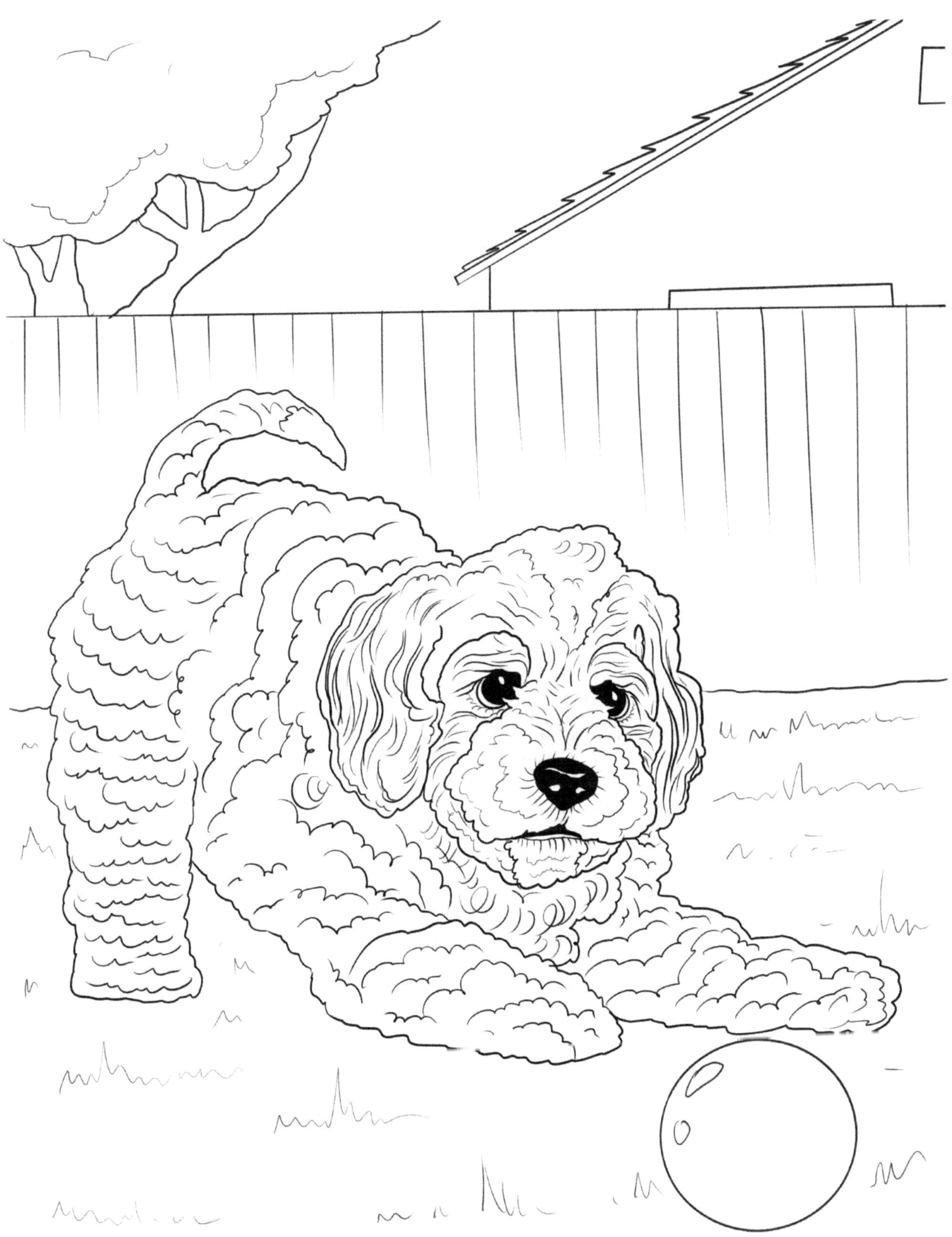

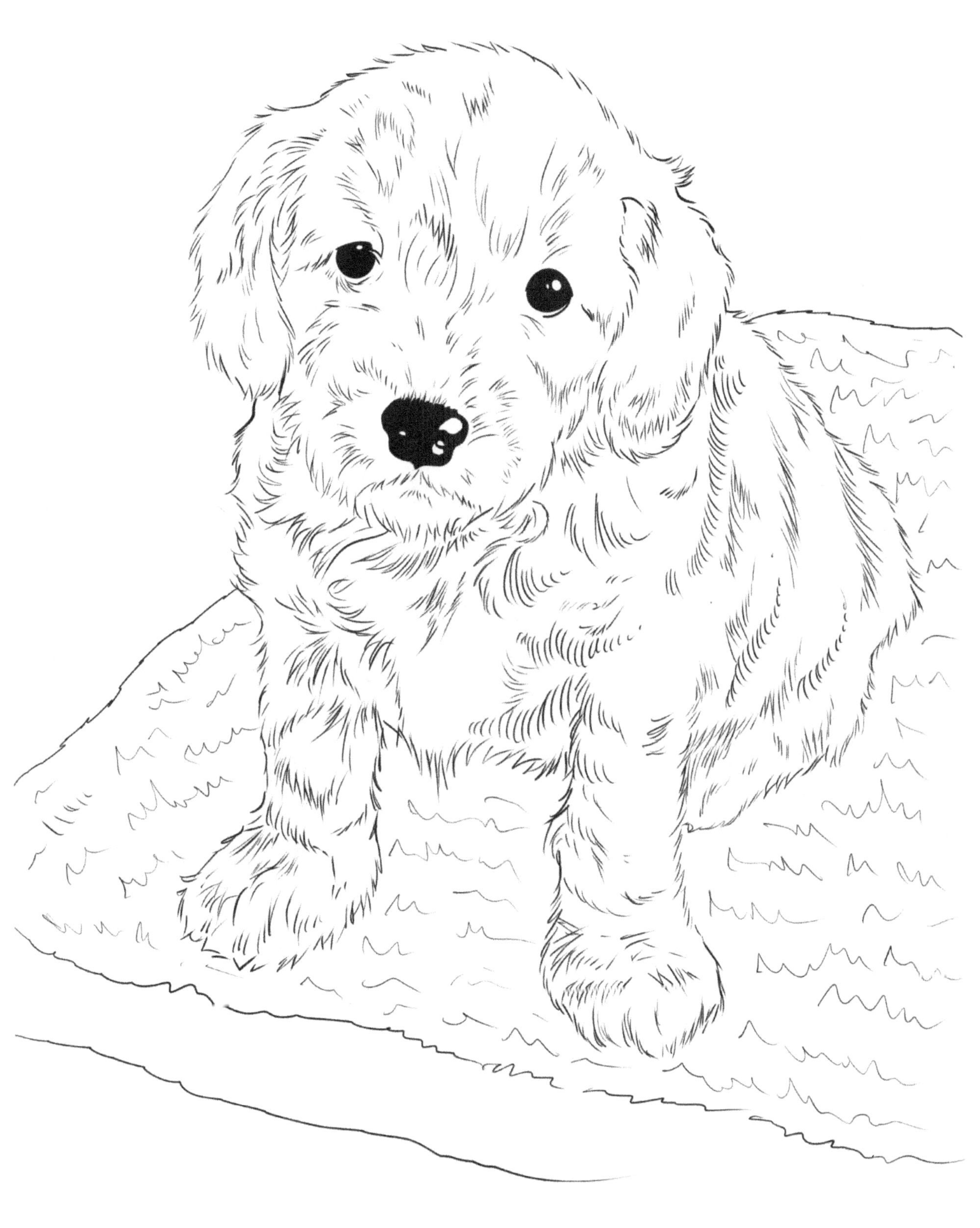

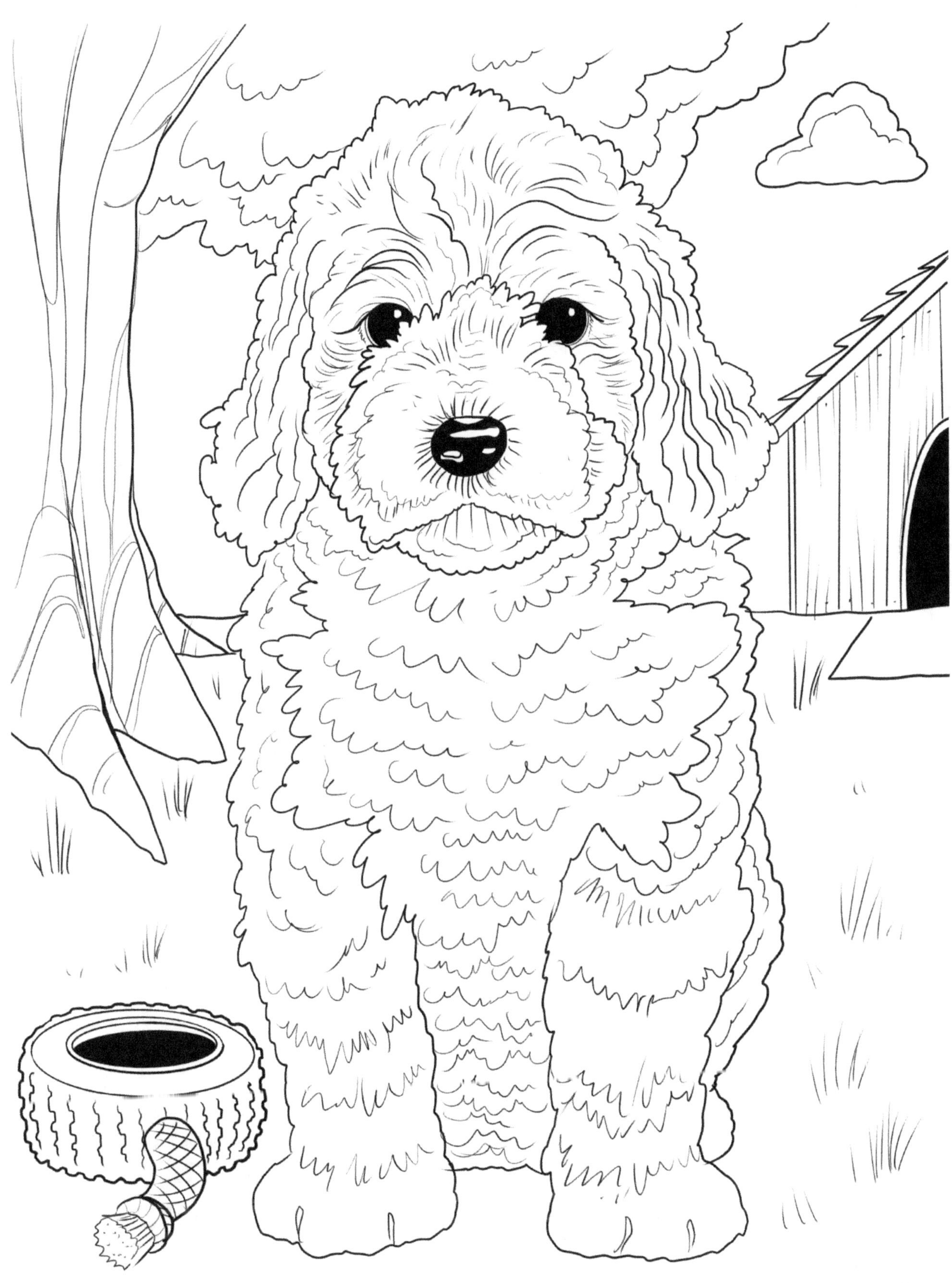

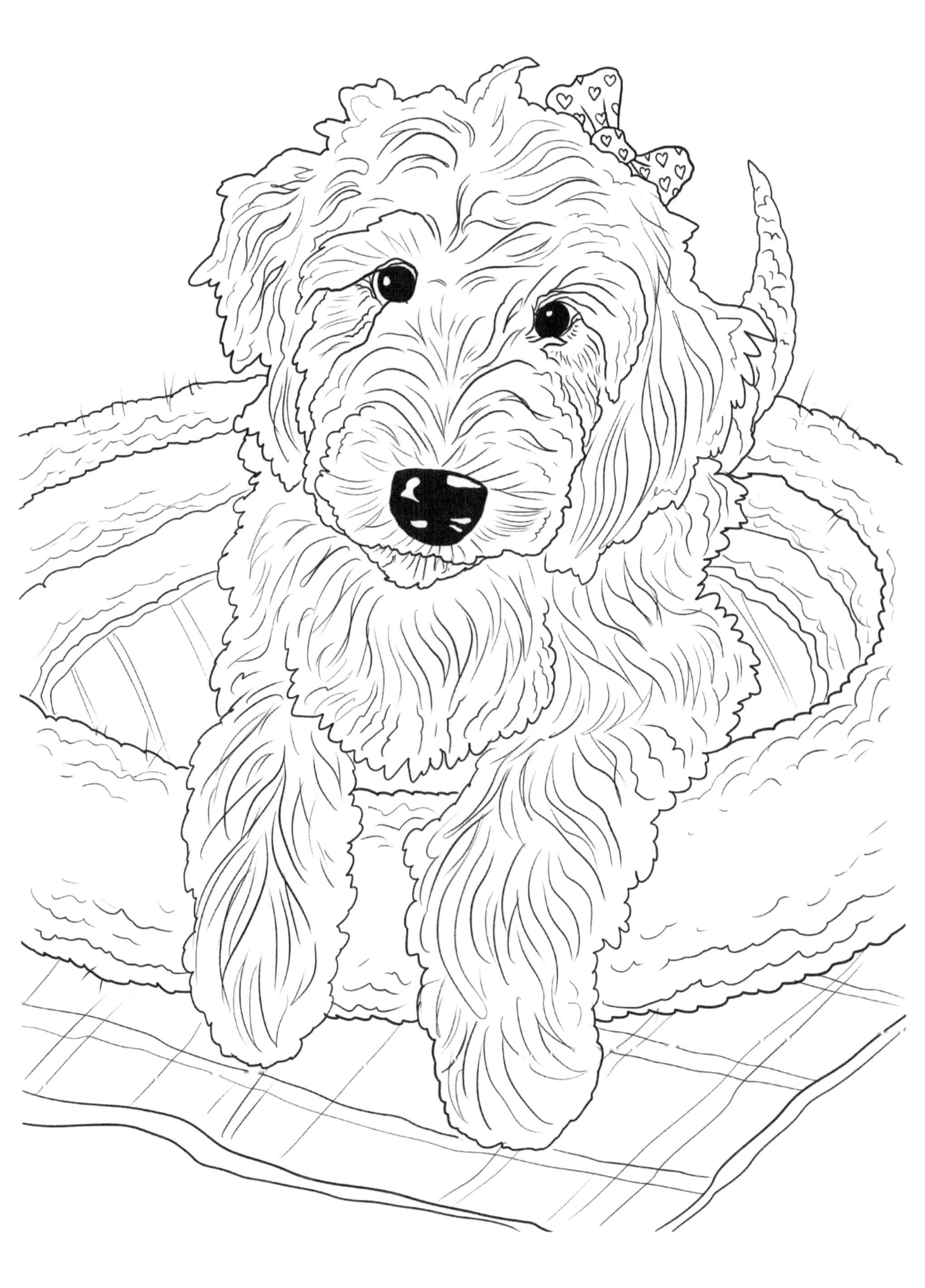

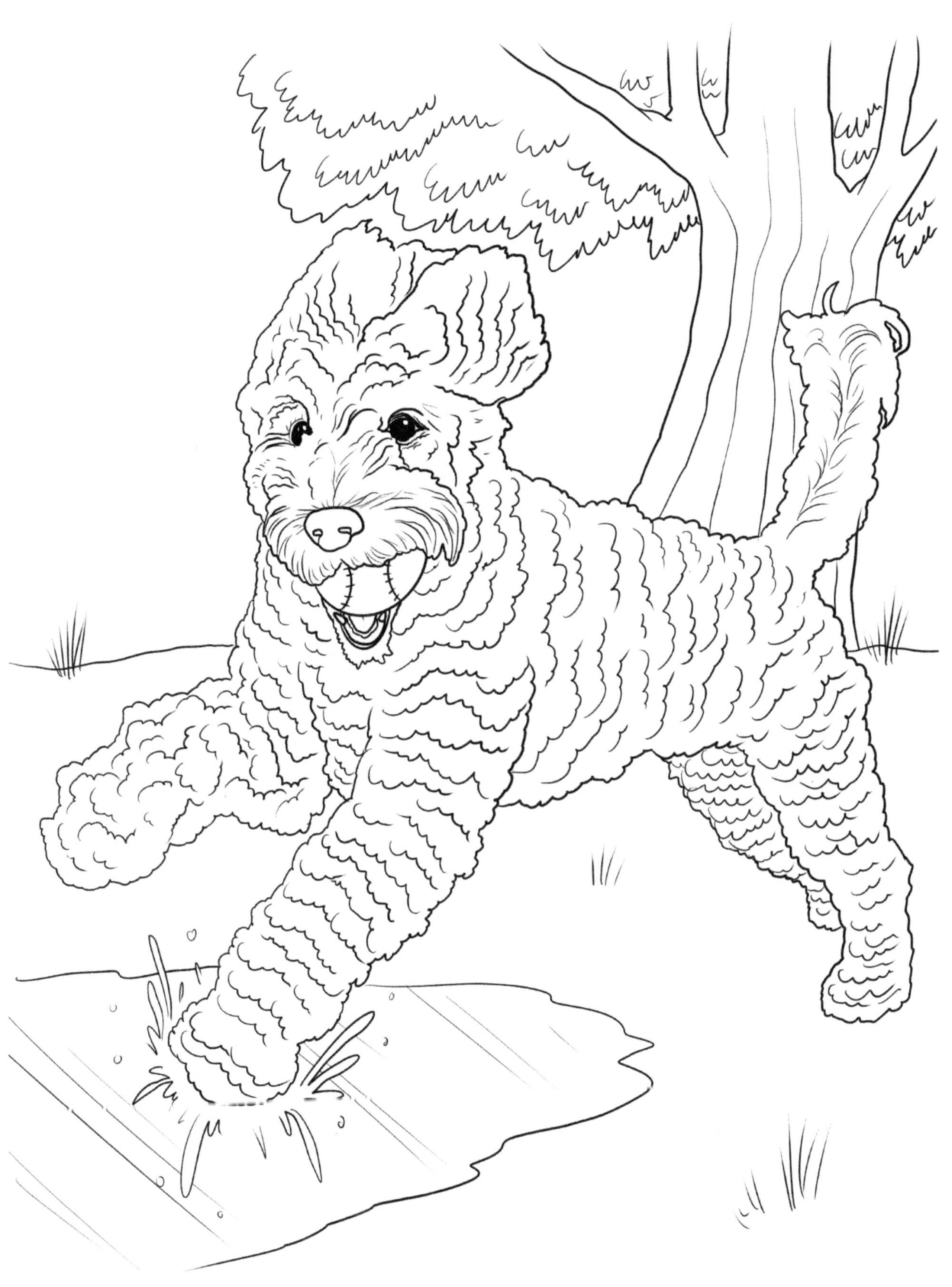

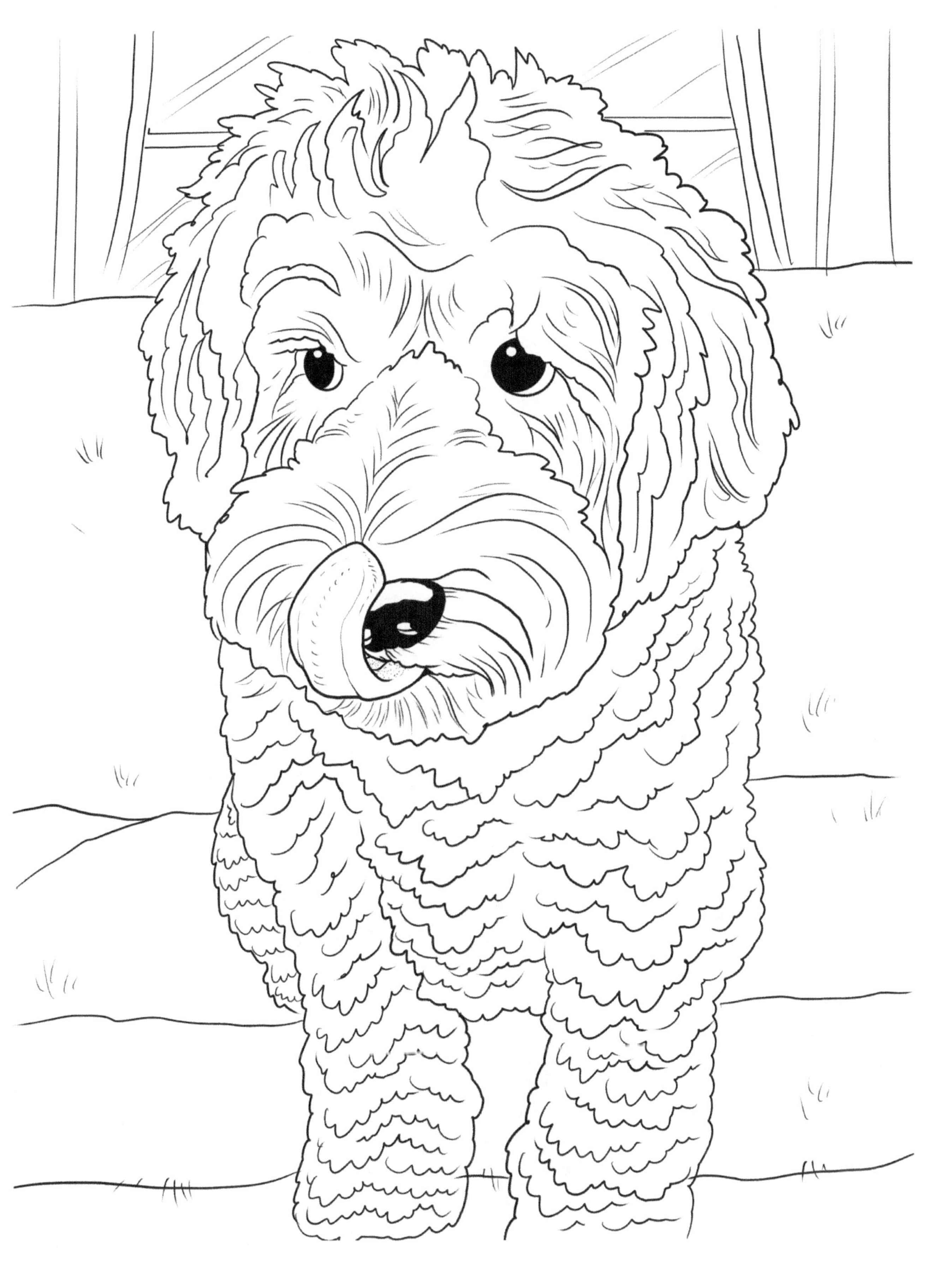

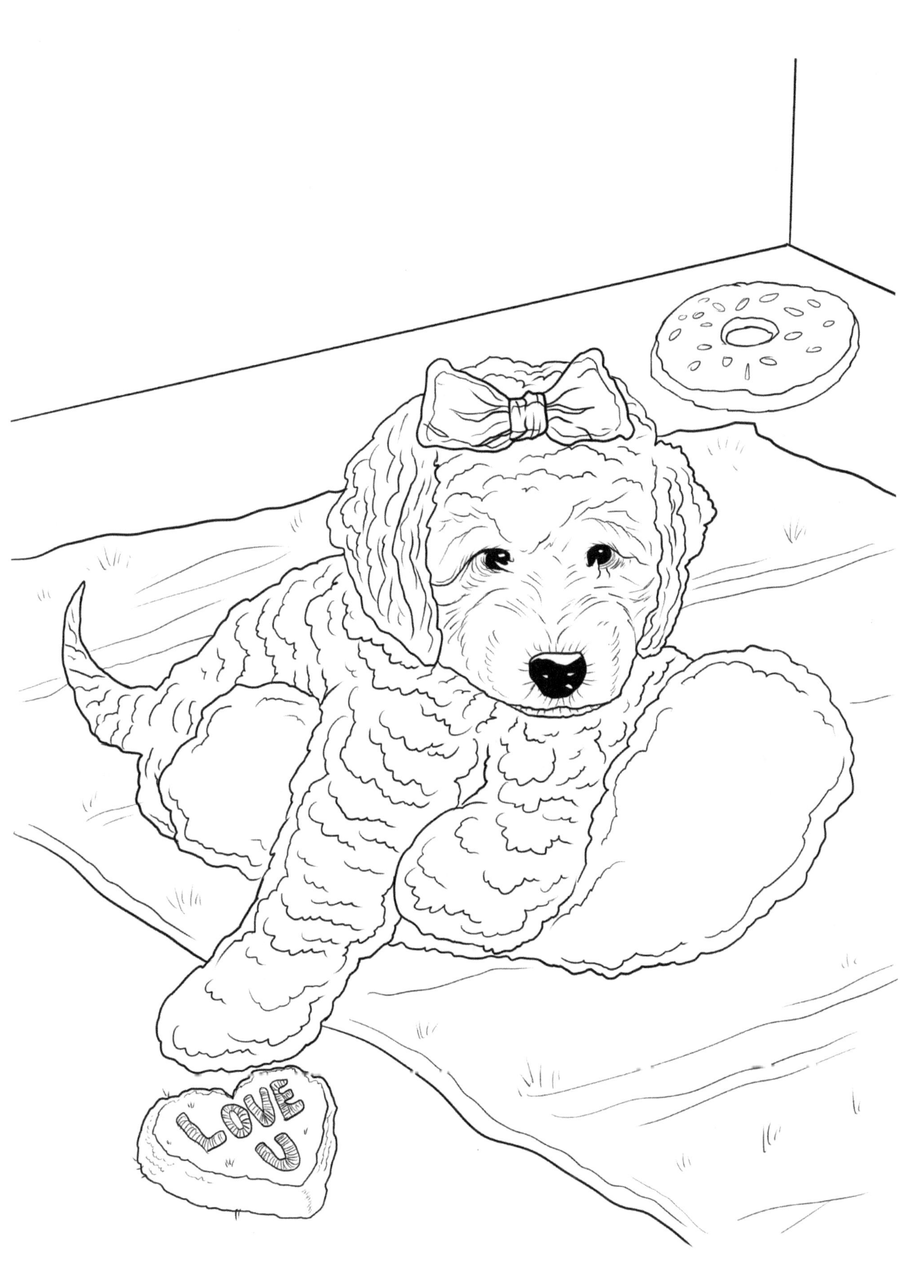

LOVE U

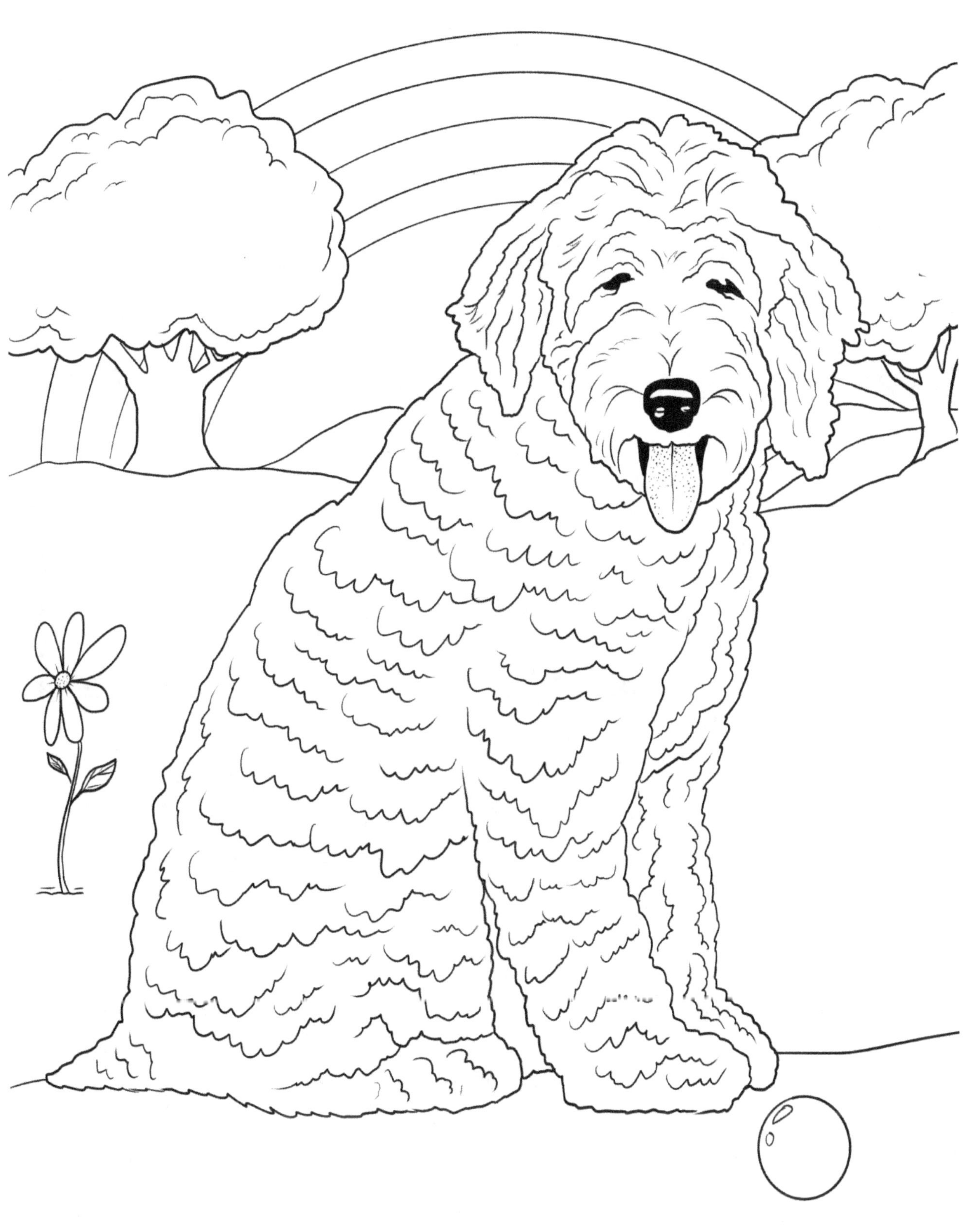

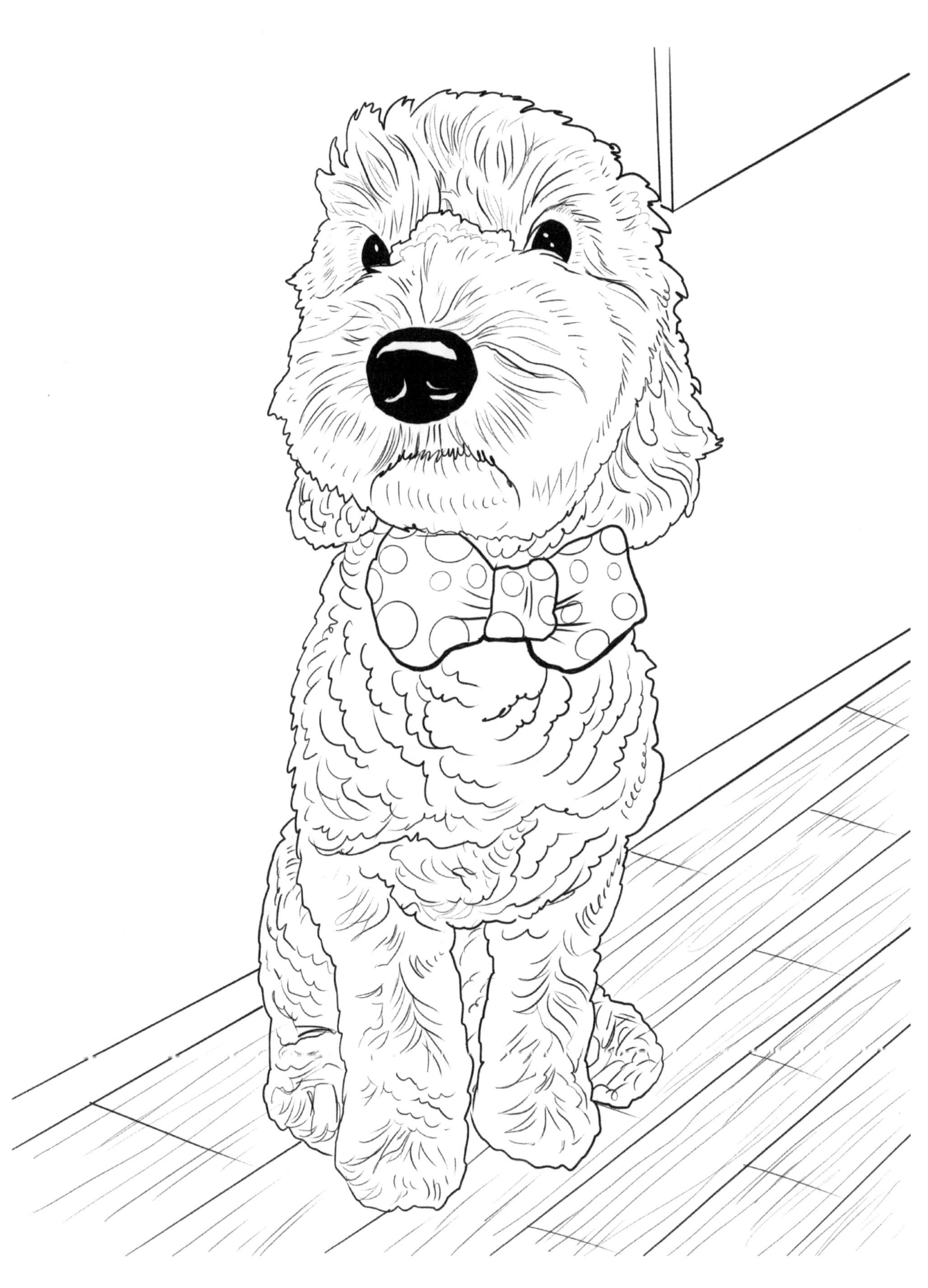

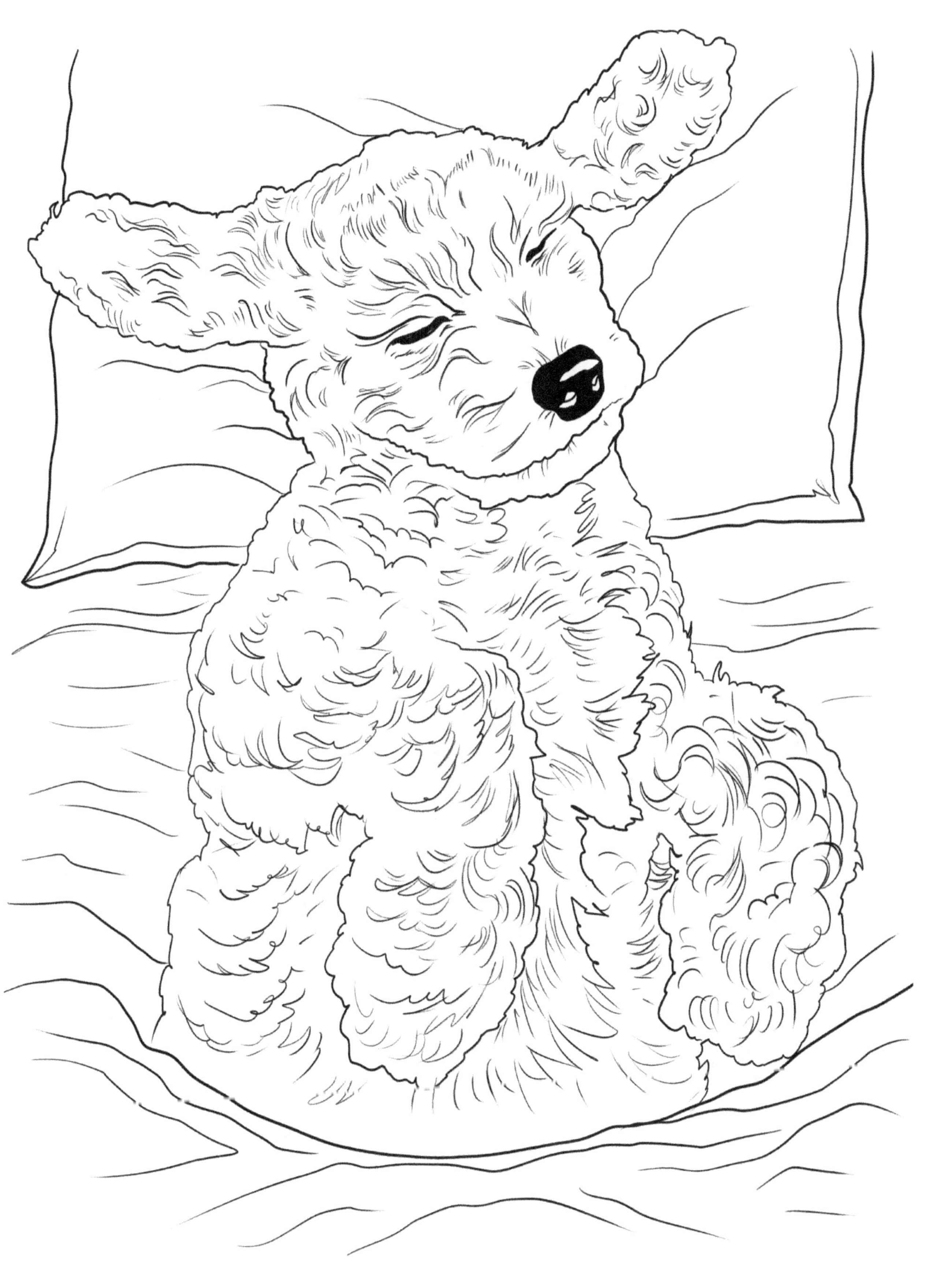

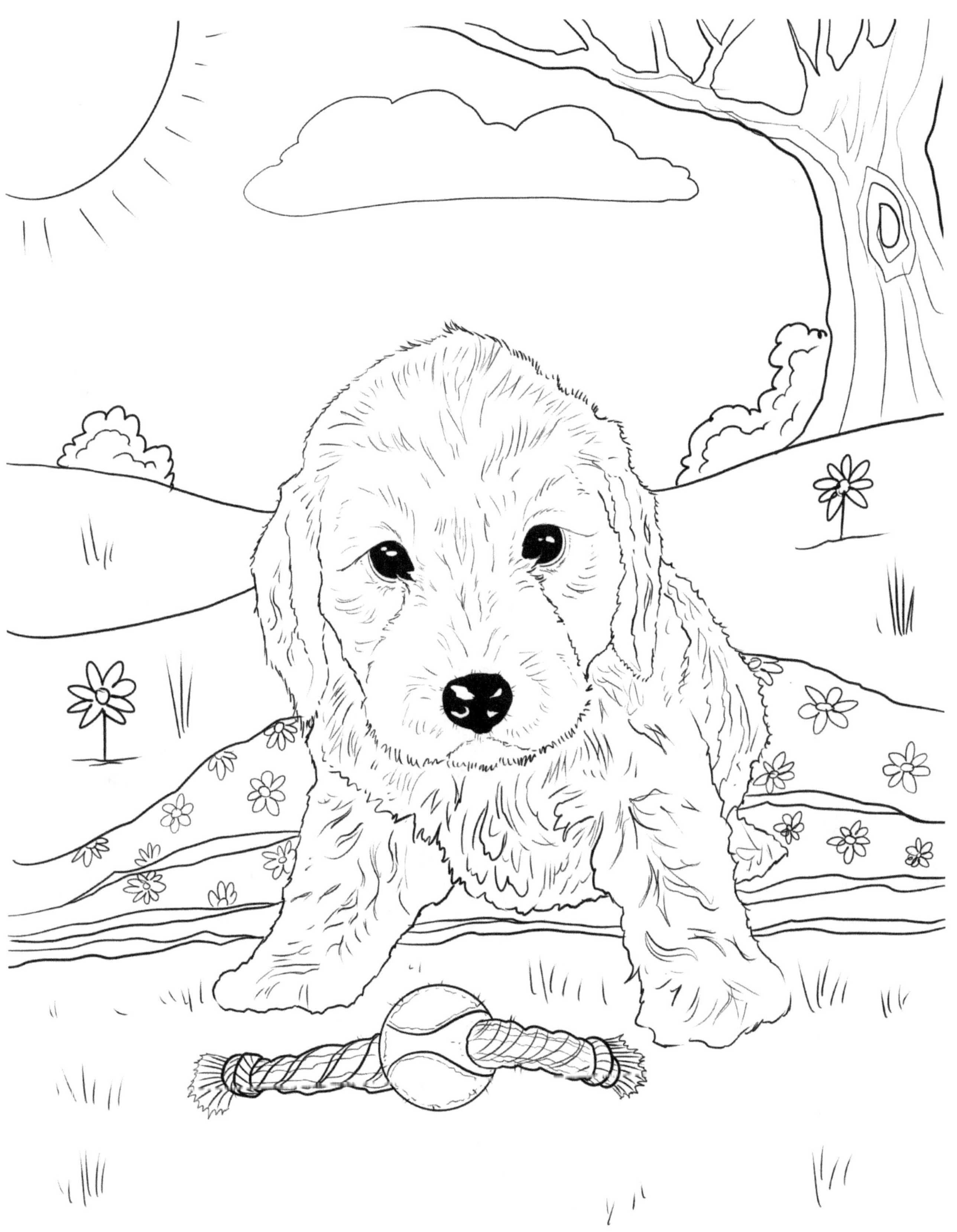

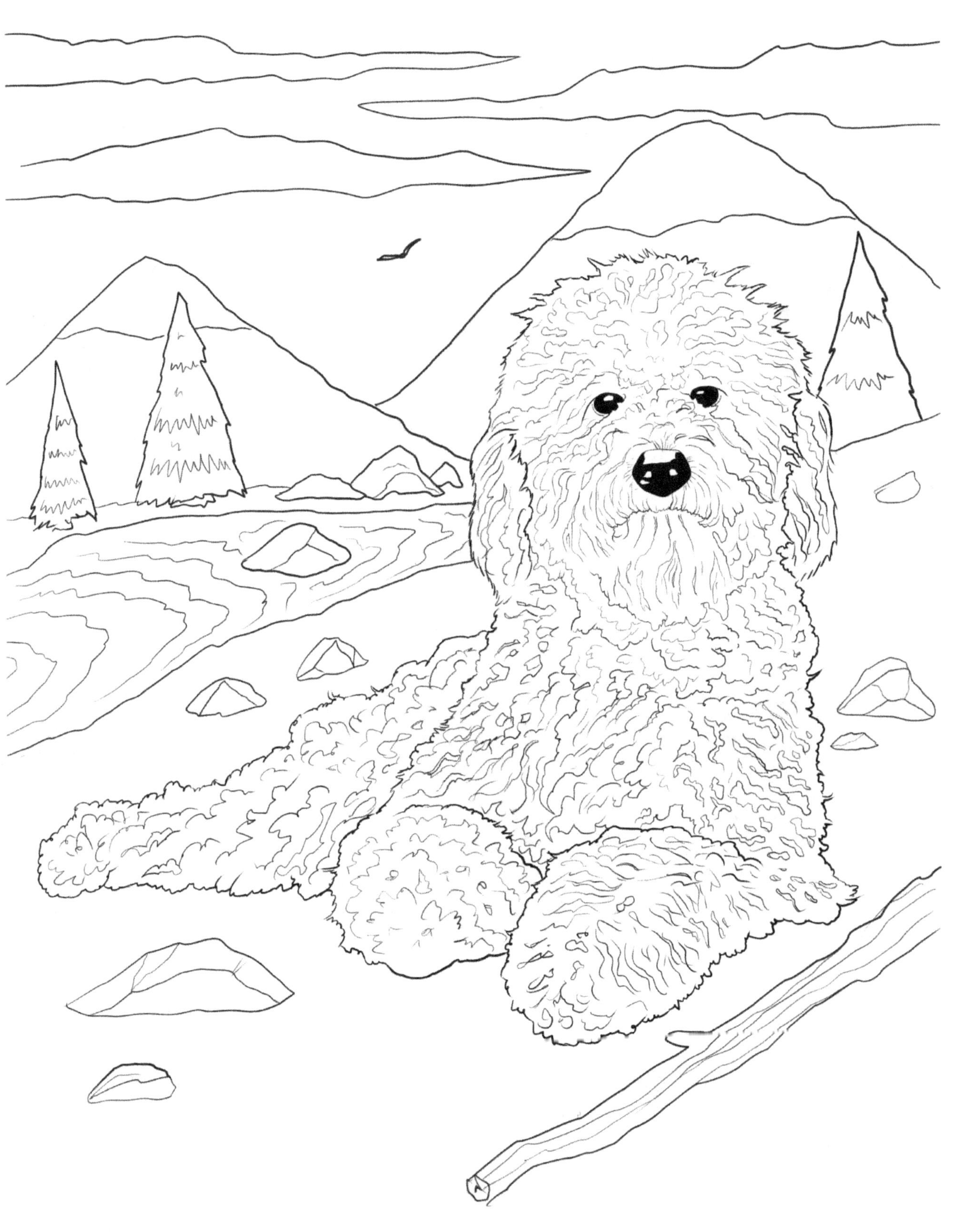

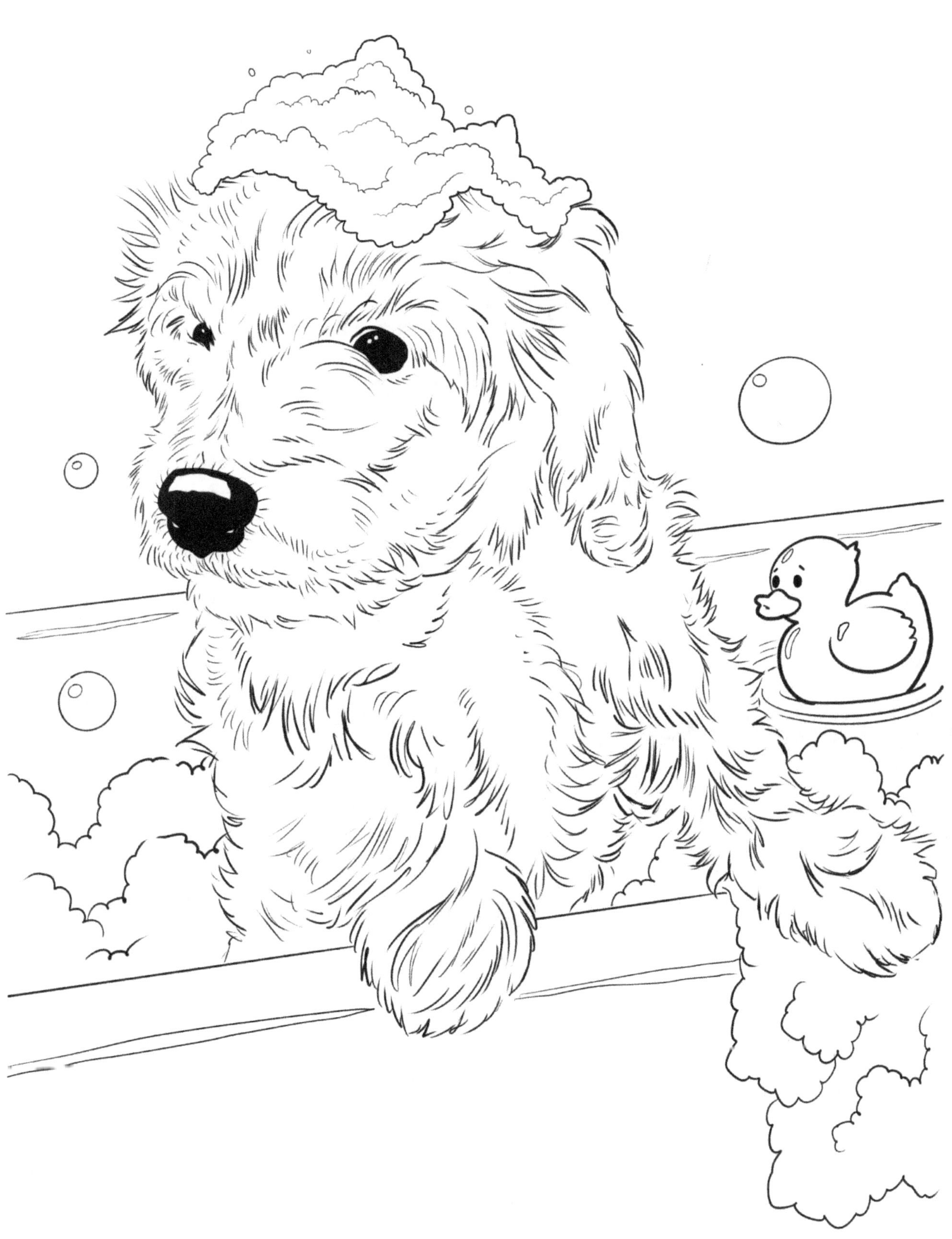

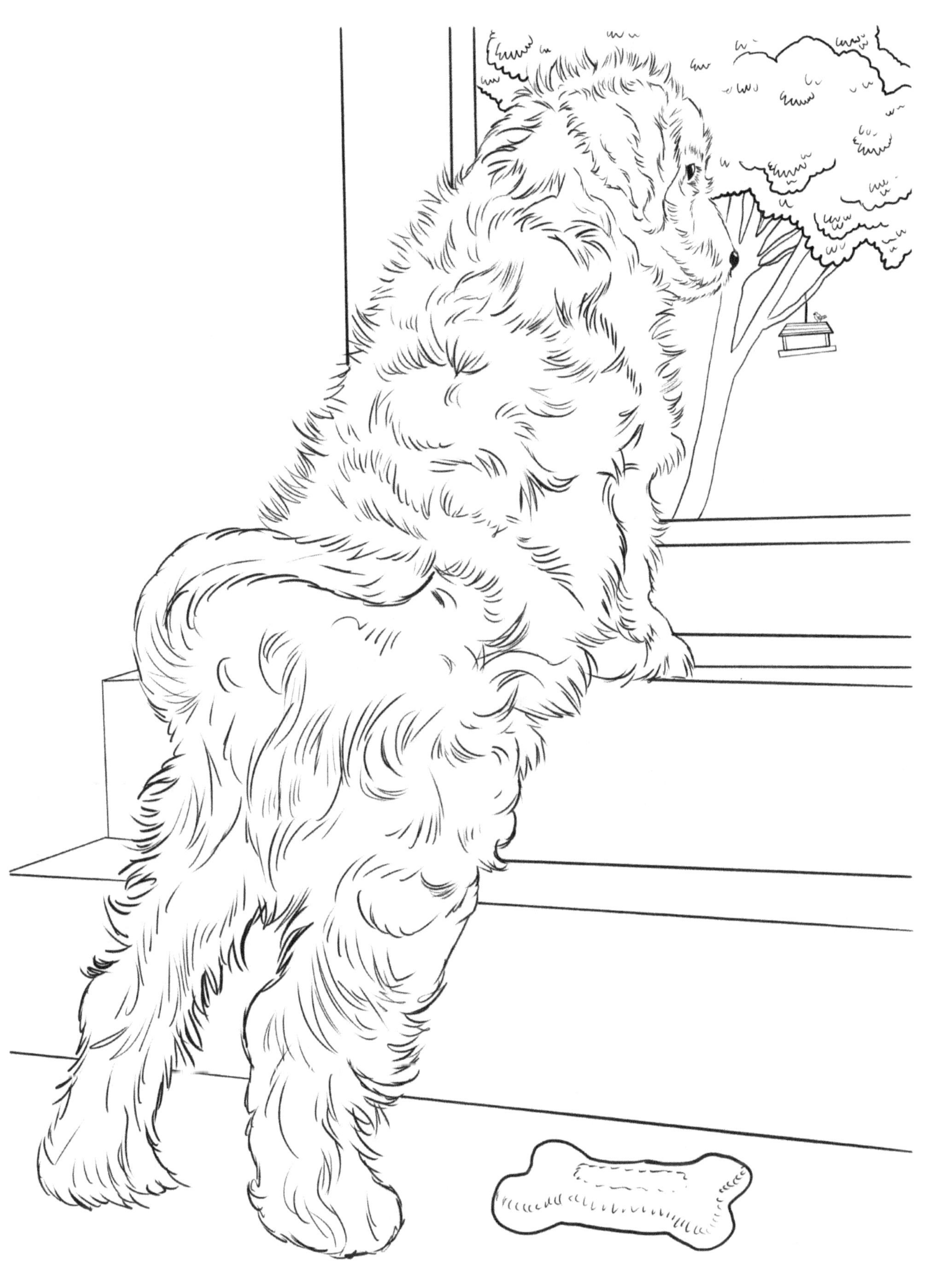

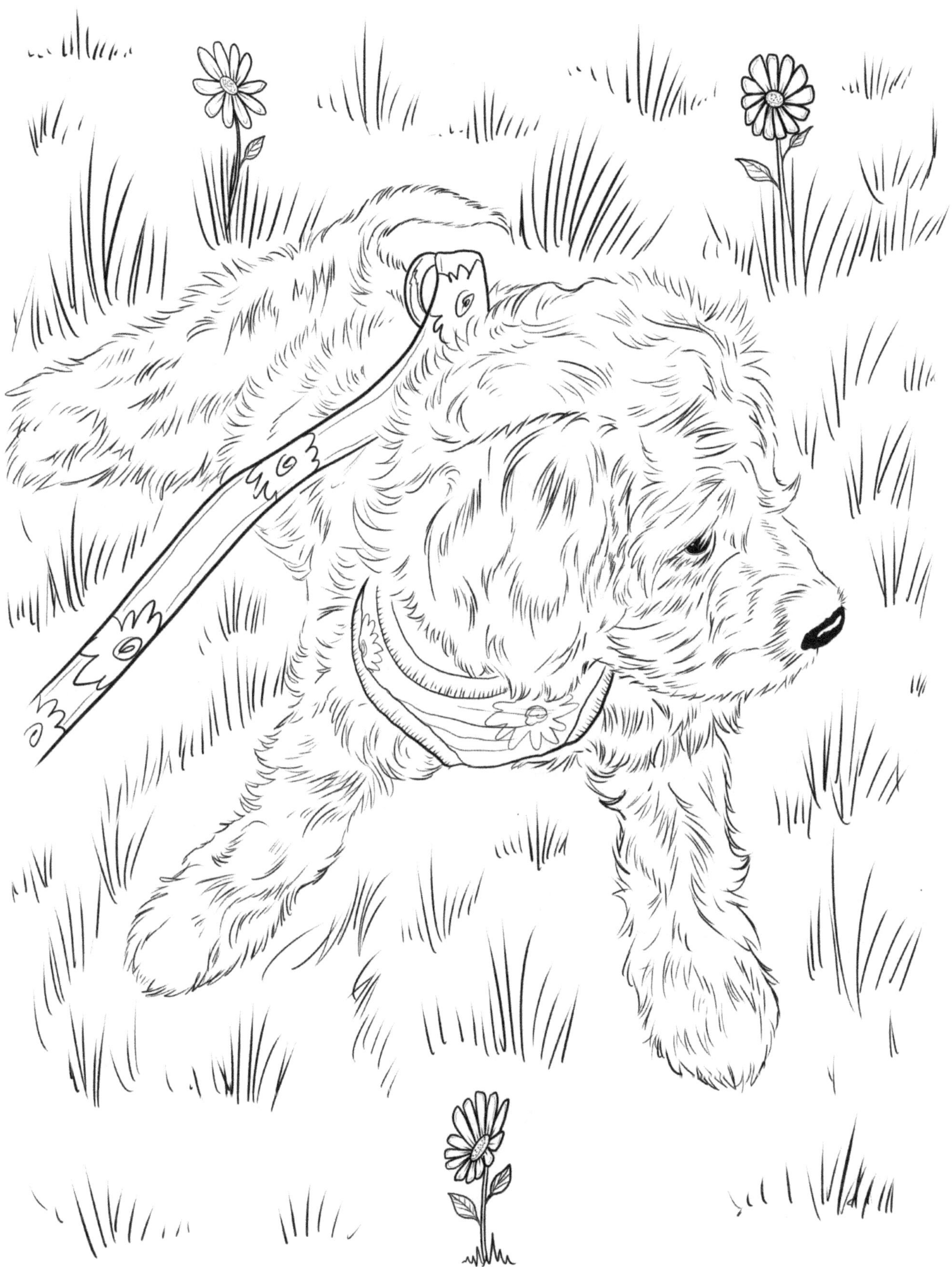

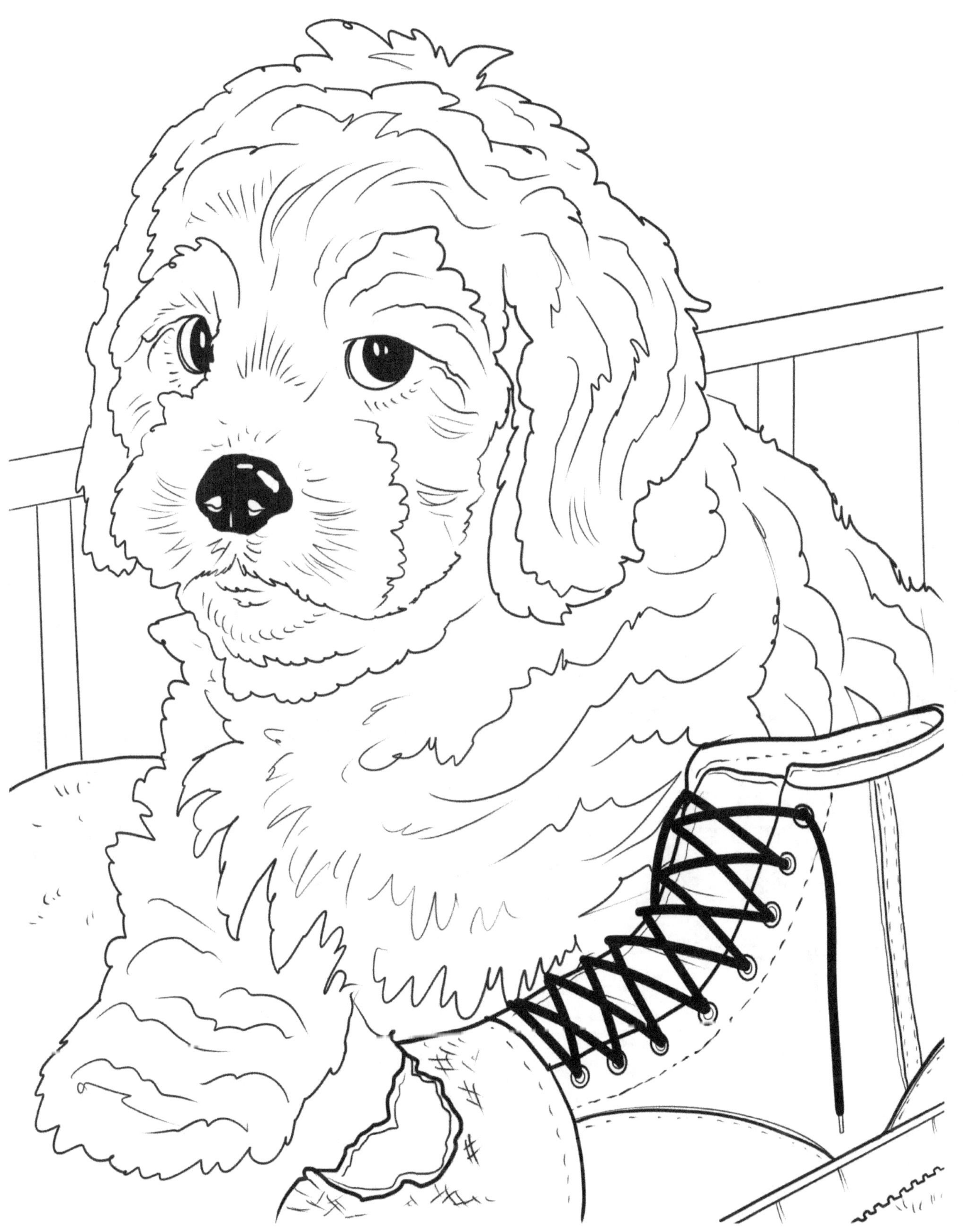

SCAN FOR MORE COLORING BOOKS BY ARTIST & CHECK BACK FOR FUTURE RELEASES!

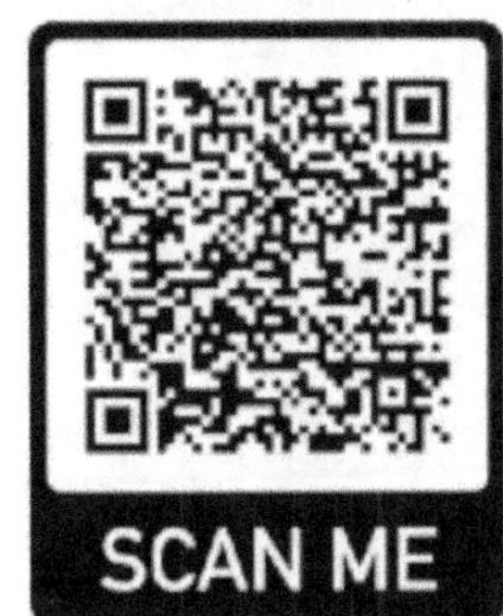

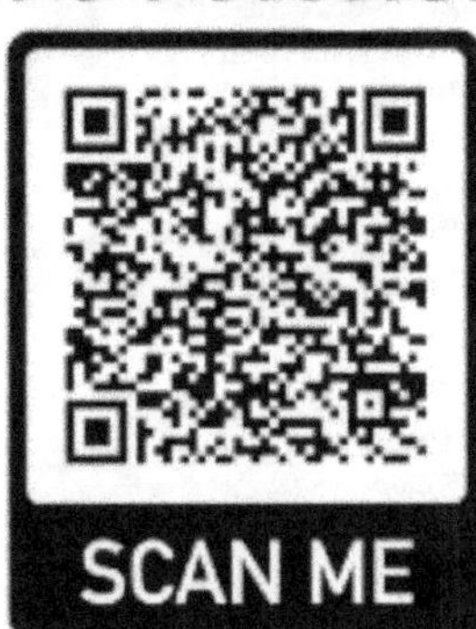

Thank You!